Praise for *Experience, Inc.*

"As an unusually dynamic leader, Jill Popelka knows that putting people first is how you build a company to last. Her engaging, user-friendly book offers the practical tools that workplaces need to bring out the best in everyone."

—Adam Grant,
#1 *New York Times* bestselling author of
Think Again and host of the TED podcast WorkLife

"Organizational scientists have well understood the linkage between employee experience and organizational effectiveness, but the gap between research and practice has left so much lost in translation. Experience, Inc. bridges the gap by breaking down the what, why, and how of employee experience in a way that is both evidence-based and actionable."

—Dr. Autumn Krauss,
Chief Scientist, SAP SuccessFactors

"Employee Experience is not an HR issue or responsibility. It is a must for every leader in the organization to foster an inspiring and desirable environment where people can unleash their full potential. If you want to be an inspiring leader, I recommend focusing on purpose, agency, belonging, and recognition. Jill, thanks for reminding us that business is all about **people***."*

—Hernan Garcia,
Head of Talent & Experience, Tecnológico de Monterrey

JILL POPELKA

EXPERIENCE, INC.

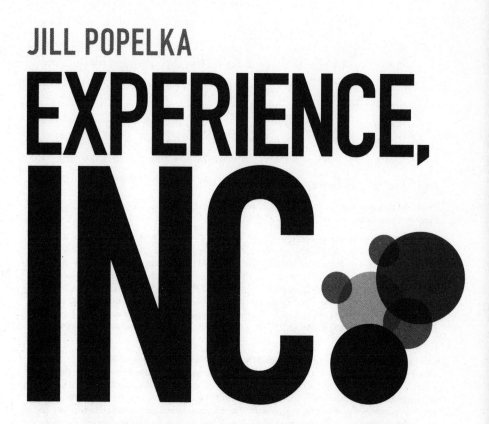

WHY COMPANIES THAT UNCOVER PURPOSE, CREATE CONNECTION, AND CELEBRATE THEIR PEOPLE WILL TRIUMPH

WILEY

For general information on our other products and services or for technical support, please contact
our Customer Care Department within the United States at (800) 762-2974, outside the United States
at (317) 572-3993 or fax (317) 572-4002.

Wiley publishes in a variety of print and electronic formats and by print-on-demand. Some material
included with standard print versions of this book may not be included in e-books or in print-on-
demand. If this book refers to media such as a CD or DVD that is not included in the version you
purchased, you may download this material at http://booksupport.wiley.com. For more information
about Wiley products, visit www.wiley.com.

Library of Congress Cataloging-in-Publication Data is Available:

ISBN 9781119852872 (Hardback)
ISBN 9781119852896 (ePDF)
ISBN 9781119852889 (ePub)

Author Photo: Photo by Madison Chaisson
Cover Design and Images: Wiley

SKY10033160_030722

First and most and above all else, I dedicate this book to my mother. She taught me to love and seek to understand others deeply, to show up and care for people, and to never give up. I have always known without any doubt that she loves me unconditionally and believes in me with her whole heart. Without her as my backstop, none of the risks I've taken in life would have been possible. She is also a great encourager on social media . . . the digital world would be a better place if we all had her spirit!

Mom was the foundation, and Dad was the inspiration. He taught me how to believe in others, to take time to think – really think – and the value of experience in learning. He always encouraged me to take the next leap, whether it was my first time riding a horse or my first international travel. When it comes to parents, I hit the jackpot, and I will be forever grateful for their investment in me.

Contents

Part III
Foundations for a Great Employee Experience

Part IV
So What?

Epilogue

Foreword

Employee Experience: It's Here to Stay

In the old days, we used to talk about keeping employees happy, paying a fair wage, and making sure our benefits were competitive. Today, however, the nature of work is changing rapidly, and workers have so many options, we have to think differently. It's time to design the employee experience that works.

As a business leader and technology innovator, Jill has had the opportunity to think deeply about the issues of experience design. And in this book, she unlocks many of the important secrets.

As my own research points out, the challenge today is not just giving employees lots of perks and programs – it's a problem of designing an entire work environment that delivers productivity, support, and growth. And each role is different, so we have to design an experience that's relevant to each job.

And as Jill discusses in the book, technology only plays a supporting role. You may believe you can "buy" employee experience from a vendor, but this is not enough. The design must include a sober look at leadership, rewards, diversity, growth, and the lived experiences of workers.

I encourage readers to use this book as a guide, a launching point, and an opportunity to think big. Employee experience must be owned by the CEO, HR team, IT team, and every single manager. If you think about the stories in this book, there are some great examples you can leverage to make your employees more included, productive, excited, and engaged.

The focus on employee experience is one of the biggest shifts in business. Let's all dive in and make work life better in our own organizations.

Josh Bersin

Global Industry Analyst and CEO,

The Josh Bersin Company

Let's Start Here

The world as we have created it is a process of our thinking. It cannot be changed without changing our thinking.

Albert Einstein

1

A Brief, Not Particularly Employee-Friendly History of Work

Consider the employee experience over the last 3,000 years.

History tells us it was harsh, usually brutal. It was tedious. Workers, including children, were often exploited or far worse. Conditions could be unbearable, with few if any safety precautions. Laborers were often unappreciated for their efforts. It was called *work* for a reason.

For thousands of years we worked from dawn until dusk. Rulers or wealthy employers established pay and taxes and could change them on a whim. You decided how much risk you would accept for the advertised reward but, for most, it was no choice at all.

During the Industrial Revolution, workers experienced a huge shift from primarily agrarian labor and the creation of hand-crafted goods to mass manufacturing, enabled by technology. People moved to cities, where growth and industry offered more reliable jobs, albeit with similarly terrible conditions. Some governments and newly formed labor unions fought to improve worker health and safety, but struggled to keep up with the dizzying pace of change. Mass production and assembly lines generated an economic boon. Though responsibilities changed, workers still faced monotonous and tiresome tasks. Your job wasn't to be happy at work; it was to do your work.

Work, and our relationship to it, has continued to evolve. Over the last 50 years, many jobs moved from the production of goods to the delivery of services. The number of professional and technical workers increased dramatically. With the rise of the knowledge worker, alongside sweeping advances in telecommunications and the emergence of the internet, work was no longer inextricably linked to a specific work*place*. Once without choice, workers began to enjoy agency for the first time.

We've come a long way.

It's Different Now

Historically, we have talked about labor markets from a supply-demand perspective. Companies managed employees as assets. In a scarce labor market, when the number of jobs exceeds the number of qualified candidates, employees have the power. In a surplus labor market, things get better for companies but worse for employees.

Is this a healthy way to think about the relationship between employees and companies? Treating it as a zero-sum battle for supremacy? Is it good for societies to talk about human beings using terms like "surplus"? This is unsustainable if we are to create a healthy society with trusted companies and happy, productive citizens.

We are starting to see a complex shift, brought on by changing global demographics, new economic norms, and advancing technologies. Employees are reevaluating the purpose of work and demanding a new set of rules. Employers are struggling to keep up.

Julia Pollak, chief economist at ZipRecruiter, says, "People don't realize the scale of what has changed. If you take even one chair away in musical chairs, it changes the entire dynamic of the game. That's what we're seeing now, where the 50 percent increase in job openings has given job seekers dramatically more leverage."[1]

On one hand, I hear from CEOs and Chief Human Resources Officers (CHROs) about their need for talent. Companies are hiring at record rates, yet simply can't fill roles fast enough.

Evolving and expanding expectations have left businesses struggling to appeal to the right candidates. Candidates see career development and talent mobility as a must. Hefty equity grants, once a luxury, are now standard. Freedom policies and remote work are expected. Even something unheard of ten years ago, like pet insurance, can be a deciding factor.

On the other hand, I hear about so many people who *can't* find a job.

What's the real story? Have we over-automated talent acquisition? Are we trying too hard to apply technology, taking the humanity out of the recruitment process? Are we overreliant on personal networks and underinvested in finding diverse voices? Are we doing a disservice to our own teams and businesses, as well as the candidates in the market?

CHROs are doing incredible work to deliver the increased employee choice and development opportunities required by candidates and employees. They are quickly innovating new tools and processes in the name of employee experience. When supported by leaders, they have done well to drive improved employee engagement and leadership trust. Despite insights from advanced analytics, the constant shifts in their workforces make it difficult to pinpoint one root cause. Even Nobel Prize-winning economists aren't sure. "The Great Resignation," writes Paul Krugman in *The New York Times*, "remains somewhat mysterious."[2]

We're witnessing many dramatic developments at once:

- new technology and the ever-increasing speed, power, and assimilation of automation, including robotics and artificial intelligence, which create new jobs while hastening the extinction of others
- greater access to information, including legislated transparency about business practices

- growing disconnect between the education and labor markets (According to the U.S. Bureau of Labor Statistics, there are one million more coding jobs in America than workers to fill them.)[3]
- the greatest public health crisis in a century and the ensuing economic fallout from the pandemic, including significant job loss and small business closures
- widespread protests over racial and economic issues, leading to greater awareness and action about social justice
- extreme political polarization and paralysis

Any one of these forces is enough to meaningfully impact the labor market and society as a whole. We find ourselves at a tumultuous, pivotal moment for business, for organizations, and for society.

I believe, and will argue in this book, that we are entering a more human-centric era for work. And that's good for business.

The Challenge and the Opportunity

What will the near future look like for the global economy and labor markets? What will it look like for individual industries? For the way we work? Of course, there's much we don't know (as the Danish physicist Niels Bohr noted, "It's difficult to make projections, particularly about the future"), but the winners of tomorrow will almost certainly be those best prepared for it. As renowned business management consultant Peter Drucker liked to say, "The best way to predict the future is to create it."

Research highlights some of the most important trends:

- *Workers – everyone – will be on the move like never before*. The average amount of time that a technical skill remains relevant is approximately five years.[4] The average American moves their place of residence 11.4 times over the course of their lifetime.[5]

- *Workers will not be office-bound or 9-to-5-bound.* Almost three in four employees said that flexible work arrangements increased their satisfaction at work; almost four in five said "flexible work arrangements made them more productive."[6] The pandemic has supercharged this.

- *Workers are fearful and unsure.* Slightly more than half of U.S. employees fear that their job will eventually be lost to automation.[7] Over half of current students in primary school will work in jobs that don't yet exist.[8] Because of the speed of technological advancement, the risk today is greater than in 1890 that workers will fall behind as work moves forward without them. Some jobs, like truck driving, will largely disappear because of the savings that automation (self-driving trucks) provides; those millions of truck drivers, it is said, will be poorly positioned for reskilling. In a fast-moving, digitally mediated labor market, how can individuals keep their skills up-to-date? Will taking a different path preclude the employee from enjoying certain professional opportunities and success?

- *Workers are overwhelmed.* Senior executives now receive 200+ emails daily.[9] The amount of new information produced in the world continues to double every 18 months.[10] So many of us suffer from "information anxiety," the fear that systems we rely on are fast outstripping our ability to comprehend and manage them.

- *Business leaders and Human Resources departments are overwhelmed.* How will companies know which mix of skills they need? Because of the sheer number of different credentials, employers struggle to understand what exactly they're looking for – not just because of uncertainty caused by technological shifts, but also because it's difficult to standardize the description of skills and jobs even across the different parts of a single organization. How can HR know that workers have truly earned the credentials they claim? And will this complicate their efforts to diversify the incoming workforce?

• *Schools are overwhelmed.* From universities to coding academies, there is similar uncertainty about what to offer, even when there's a strong desire to teach to near-term market demands.

• *Parents are overwhelmed.* Whether it's the need for childcare or their kids falling behind in competing in the global economy, parents feel fear and uncertainty about what may lie ahead.

In my role as president of SAP SuccessFactors, I see countless companies struggling with these changing dynamics and competing forces. How could they not?

My team has access to research and data that allow us to spot organizational and industry trends. This is what we see: Employee experience has become a business imperative. It's not something that companies can say they would "like to do better." To survive or thrive, it's required.

For as long as there has been business, there has been a focus on growing revenue, capitalizing on new markets and customers, and innovating faster than competitors. Finding high-performing, highly skilled employees was up there, too. But truly engaging employees – helping people to have a work experience that fulfills them – was not.

Now it is.

Employee experience should be at the top of the priority list. It is the dimension by which all other business objectives will be met. If businesses don't elevate its importance in today's world, they will struggle to compete.

This book will focus on the principles around employee experience. It will not provide a magic formula. But my belief is that by having the key issues in mind, business leaders can begin to solve their design problem: how to create a superior environment for workers, one that helps them to recruit and hire the best talent, retain it, and have them work productively and innovatively. This is a leadership issue, not a Human Resources issue. It's not something that can be delegated or relegated. Nothing could be more important for those hoping to compete in the global market of the future.

The realist out there might be thinking: *I've got too much going on as it is. Now is not the time to follow the next fad.*

Or you may wonder: *Can I seriously take the time to focus on employee experience and still meet my business results?*

Absolutely. Investing in employee experience makes everyone's lives easier and more rewarding. For employees, customers, and leaders. Get this right and your company has an opportunity to lap the field.

This book brings together insights from my own experience, as an employee and a leader; SAP's work with thousands of customers; our extensive, ongoing research on the subject of employee experience; outside research; and interviews we've conducted with managers and employees, at various levels, industries, and regions – in technology, finance, medicine, education, retail, construction, media, design, law, and more.

For businesses to succeed in the coming years, they need to understand the issues around employee experience and address them, because a new era is here. It's great for the employee, and way past time. It's also great for employers and businesses, because improved employee experience translates to an improved bottom line.

What is it that employees want more than anything? We've known for decades that good working conditions are necessary to attract and retain talent. Fair compensation, a safe and stable environment, career growth. All of that is sufficient to attract and retain talent in the current economy – but not enough. Smart companies and good leaders need to fully engage and unleash people's potential. To do that, leaders must go beyond the basics of good working conditions to provide four pillar notions. These are based on our findings, from working with customers and dedicated research, and have been corroborated by others.

So, what *do* employees want?

Purpose. Agency. Belonging. Recognition.

- **Purpose:** to find meaning in their work
- **Agency:** to have some say over how, when, and where they work
- **Belonging:** to feel part of a community, even if they are remote, freelance, or part-time; to be part of a diverse community
- **Recognition:** to be acknowledged for their contributions, in multiple forms, on a regular basis

You have some history and current context. I've outlined the key needs and wants of employees. Now, let's get to the important points around employee experience, and why nothing matters more to the future of your company.

Employee Experience

The New Why

" I hate the word 'experience,'" the CHRO of a global consumer products company told me. "It's difficult to define and there's no way my CFO will pay for it."

What Exactly *Is* "Employee Experience"?

I get what she's saying. For many leaders, investing resources to plan and create an outstanding employee experience may seem difficult to justify. After all, how do you convert purpose, agency, belonging, and recognition into goals? What would you measure? How does it align with business outcomes? How would you budget for it? Who would determine if you've succeeded?

A useful definition of employee experience comes from my colleague at SAP, Dr. Steve Hunt, an industrial-organizational psychologist who has explored this topic through his work with more than a thousand companies around the globe. "'Employee experience' refers to the beliefs, feelings, attitudes, and behaviors resulting from one's job experiences," says Steve. "Three basic types of experiences influence how people feel about work."

- *Task experience: Is it easy to get things done?* This is about providing employees with the tools and resources they need to accomplish their goals at work. Good task experiences make employees feel efficient and productive; bad task experiences create frustration and a sense that the company doesn't appreciate the employee's time or skills.
- *Social experience: Do I like the people I work with and how we work together?* Creating effective team climates

and shared norms and values that support business results. Good social experiences make employees feel welcomed, included, effective, and supported. Bad social experiences make employees feel isolated, alienated, unproductive, and annoyed.

- *Fulfillment experience: Does my job provide the things I want from work?* Work can provide fulfillment in different ways. It may allow employees to achieve goals outside of work, such as providing for their families. It may give employees the opportunity to do work they enjoy, help them fulfill professional career goals, or enable them to achieve some higher-level purpose related to improving society or the planet.

Steve elaborates: "An employee's experience of fulfillment depends to some degree on all of these factors. But the importance of each factor varies across employees. The ideal job provides a positive task, social, and fulfillment experience. But few, if any, jobs are ideal. So employees make trade-offs between these experiences. It's easier to do a relatively unfulfilling job if we work with people we enjoy. We are willing to overcome bad task experiences if we believe in the purpose of our work. On the other hand, if any one of these experiences falls below a certain level for an extended amount of time, then jobs become unpleasant, stressful, and often intolerable."

Employee experience impacts purpose, agency, belonging, and recognition. A bad task experience hurts your agency – it undermines your ability to do what you need to do to be successful. A bad social experience often makes you feel uncared for and unwanted. And an unfulfilling job, by definition, is one that does not give you a sense that your work is meaningful and purposeful. You can feel unappreciated in all three types of experience: The company doesn't appreciate the value of your time (task), doesn't appreciate who you are as a person (social), or doesn't appreciate what you want to achieve in your career (fulfillment).

Here's another analogy I like to use, about one of my favorite experiences: hiking. Task experience is like having boots that fit. A hike will not be good simply because your boots fit. But if your boots don't fit, then the hike will be frustrating and potentially miserable.

Social experience is about whom you're hiking with. Do you all get along, enjoy each other's conversation, and walk at the same general pace?

Fulfillment experience is about where you're hiking to. Are you hiking through a beautiful valley to a lake you've always wanted to see, walking around a suburban neighborhood, or trudging through a mosquito-infested swamp?

Whether the hike is good or bad depends on all three of these elements. But if any single one falls below a certain level, the hike will be terrible.

For a business, the results that derive from positive employee experiences are not always direct but they are profound and provable. A nurturing and purposeful environment alters employee beliefs and attitudes. This translates to changes in employee behavior. And that benefits the bottom line. When the company creates a positive "organizational climate" – a concept from psychology, describing an environment that reflects beliefs, attitudes, and behavioral norms shared across people in a group – it influences sales revenue, customer satisfaction scores, manufacturing productivity, product quality, patient care, safety incidents, security breaches, employee well-being, equity and inclusiveness, and other metrics that impact company profit and growth. Furthermore, when you create such an appealing organizational climate, talented people who are outside the tent want to come join you inside it.

A company that does not put its employees first, whose workers are figuratively hiking through a swamp in ill-fitting boots, with people whose presence they don't enjoy: That's a business with serious problems.

What Employees Want

To attract the best employees, you must provide a great employee experience. How do you achieve that?

Two in three U.S. employees say that the most important issue for CEOs to communicate is the company's values.[1] Seven in ten employees say that leadership's stance on social issues influences whether they stay in their current job.[2] Nearly three in four claim that their principal driver is "work that has purpose and meaning."[3] And nine in ten executives believe that an organization with shared purpose will enjoy employee satisfaction.[4] The demand for meaningful, purposeful work has never been stronger than it is today.

Is compensation suddenly not important? Of course it is – though in one survey, the portion of workers who say that pay is most important is only 19 percent.[5] There will inevitably be significant differences in how much people say they are motivated by money; salespeople will answer differently from social workers. Compensation is a huge influence on our willingness to accept and remain in a job, even if it is not that important to us in the day-to-day work. What's more, the issue of money can be a huge *de*-motivator for anyone who feels they are being paid unfairly.

It's not just about purpose and meaning, though. Opportunities for learning and a breadth of career development in a professional job are among the top reasons given for remaining with a company.[6] In fact, one study found that 94 percent of employees say they would stay at a company longer if they had learning opportunities.[7] Three-quarters of employees say they are more motivated to improve their technical and professional skills as a result of the pandemic.[8]

Our fundamental psychology has not changed all that much. What made our grandparents happy at work is the same for us: achieving meaningful things in an organization where we are appreciated, valued, and feel a sense of belonging. What *has* changed is the environment we live in. What has changed is our ability to get the things that make us happy at work.

And a lot of people out there are not happy.

A staggering number of people are quitting their jobs without immediately looking for the next one – a phenomenon in the United States and elsewhere that's been dubbed (in the U.S., anyway) "The Great Resignation," creating an unpredictable labor market. "I don't want to make the same mistakes, where I just take anything, because I could end up in an even worse situation," says Kara,* formerly a project manager at a software company, voicing a common concern. "Now that I have an idea of what's out there, I don't want to jump into a brand-new role just yet." Companies are worried about recruitment and retention, about compensation and perks, and whether their efforts will succeed in this new landscape. Working conditions at a given company, bad or good, are public knowledge. "Amazon built cutting-edge package processing facilities to cater to shoppers' appetite for fast delivery, far outpacing competitors," reports *The New York Times*. "But the business did not devote enough resources and attention to how it served employees, according to many longtime workers."[9]

---

*The names of those interviewed for this book have been changed, occasionally along with minor details, to free them to speak candidly. I am grateful to all who participated and shared their insights.

Burnout, a key indicator for quitting, is rampant. Among tech workers, 58 percent report experiencing it.[10] Lots of employees – and former employees – are prioritizing that ever-elusive "work-life balance."

Companies are starting to address employee experience, but it's not easy given that they're already dealing with the challenge of the hybrid workplace. What are the new working policies? What do employees really need? How do leaders meet those individual wants and expectations if they oversee a company of 100,000? Or even just 100? Business leaders and CHROs alike face a challenge.

"I know they want to create a better experience," says Rachel, a copywriter and brand developer, about the mid-sized design firm she left for a better opportunity, "but I don't think they really know how."

Keeping Pace

For those in positions of leadership, it may feel daunting to try to manage the pace of change today. But we all know it's necessary in order to stay relevant and succeed. Because people change. Society changes. Constantly. On a recent trip to Washington, D.C., with my daughter, Kalie, I came across these words etched in stone: "Laws and institutions must go hand in hand with the progress of the human mind. As that becomes more developed, more enlightened, as new discoveries are made, new truths disclosed, and manners and opinions change with the change of circumstances, institutions must advance also, and keep pace with the times." Thomas Jefferson said that more than two centuries ago, and it's still true today.[11] Companies and their practices must change to keep pace with the progress of the human mind.

It's hard to argue that the changes in work from thousands of years ago to a century ago were greater than what we've experienced in just the last two generations, or the last five years. The word disruption has been overused, yet it accurately describes what has been going on for the last decade and even more recently. Business leaders have seen a massive reorientation around the notion of work.

Your work life was once far less flexible. Today, there's more choice, thus companies need to compete harder for your attention and loyalty. Since 1972, average gross domestic product (GDP) per capita around the globe has increased more than tenfold, which translates to more personal discretionary spending, which means more people who are able and willing to tolerate a few months out of work looking for their next job.[12] Many people are no longer satisfied simply by reaching the base levels of Maslow's iconic hierarchy pyramid – physiological (food, shelter, etc.) and safety/security (employment, social stability, etc.). They want to scale the upper levels, right to the top of the pyramid: self-actualization.

Who – during the Great Depression – would have thought that self-actualization was something to expect from one's job? Work was about a steady paycheck. Now, more people are willing and able to make trade-offs. *Do I want to spend x more hours making y more money? Or do I want to spend more time meditating?* "What if paid work is not the only worthwhile use of one's time?" *The New York Times'* Farhad Manjoo ponders. "What if crushing it in your career is not the only way to attain status and significance in society?"[13]

People want and need to feel fairly compensated and secure in their job. But people today are increasingly interested in moving around, changing jobs; résumés read like novellas. If employees are unhappy at work, they can leave.

Maybe they want to do good, or more good, or see a bigger picture, or they're no longer willing to feel like a cog in the machine.

Companies can't expect to attract the best talent, and therefore grow and succeed, without examining what they're offering. "Businesses have to understand that they need to attract and work with people in a different way if they expect to keep us," says Mark, an executive who just returned from four years in Asia. "I'm happy to be back in the San Francisco Bay area but I can work anywhere in the world. I have a talent set and I have a network. If I had an offer for a job back in Asia, I wouldn't have to move there to do it."

Leaders must think more purposefully about how they're helping their people. Today's worker will not be won over easily by empty corporate campaigns or initiatives that offer perks like foosball tables in the breakroom, ostensibly to improve their experience. These gimmicks might get you a better rating on workplace surveys but, as much psychological research shows, if companies are not offering something meaningful, they will fail. Genuine improvements in the work environment are those that affect *intrinsic* motivation and allow the worker to contribute and have a voice. These are much more predictive of employee fulfillment and business success. Some forward-looking companies are redefining their HR processes to focus more on human experience management (e.g., aspiration, work style, growth) rather than its previous focus, human capital management.

We're in the midst of a societal renegotiation. Those in a position of power must provide a better roadmap for how to engage and reward everyone. As machines get smarter and more ubiquitous, how do we ensure – or, in some senses, restore – humanity in the workplace?

Yet technological advancement is just one reason for the improvements in the way employees work and the way they are treated. In August 2019, Business Roundtable, the respected association of CEOs of America's leading companies, announced that "shareholder capitalism" was dead, replaced by "stakeholder capitalism." For more than 20 years, Business Roundtable had issued proclamations on the raison d'être of the corporation, and the shareholder was viewed always as the most important constituent. Finally, Business Roundtable changed its tune. "Major employers are investing in their workers and communities because they know it is the only way to be successful," said Jamie Dimon, CEO of J.P. Morgan Chase & Co. and then Chairman of Business Roundtable.[14]

It's interesting that it took until 2019 to formally elevate the status of workers and others, but better late than never. While "stakeholders" is a large collection (it comprises customers, employees, suppliers, communities, and shareholders), conscientious leaders understand that no one should rank higher than the worker – for humane reasons *and* business reasons. The day-to-day, lived employment experience of workers is inextricably connected to the success of their company.

It has become clear that the things employees value most from a job are no longer mere wants, but expectations. The employee feels that the employer should be involved, even responsible, for their well-being; offer learning opportunities; listen to workers; and speak out on social issues. The employee wants to find a sense of purpose in a workplace that's productive for and welcoming to everyone.

The World Economic Forum's 2020 report on Talent/ Human Capital framed the reset of values in the new world of work.[15] This included moving from a process-centric "Employees and Jobs" focus to a more human-centric "People, Work, and Skills" focus.

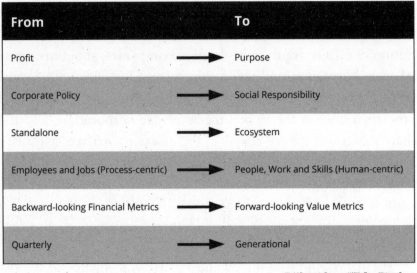

From	To
Profit	Purpose
Corporate Policy	Social Responsibility
Standalone	Ecosystem
Employees and Jobs (Process-centric)	People, Work and Skills (Human-centric)
Backward-looking Financial Metrics	Forward-looking Value Metrics
Quarterly	Generational

World Economic Forum and Willis Tower Watson: Seven guiding principles to shift how human capital is valued

The World Economic Forum has also established a set of recommended metrics for businesses, to help drive sustainability as it relates to people. The themes are Dignity and Equality, Health and Well-being, and Skills for the Future. As companies strive to be more sustainable, it will be important that they also focus on a shared future.

Leaders know they must deliver. In a 2020 *Forbes* survey, the heads of Human Resources and other departments were asked to name their top initiatives. The top answer, ranked first by half the respondents, was employee experience.[16]

Getting It Right

The world of work has changed, and leaders need to manage differently not just to attract and retain talent but also to create and recreate high-performing, adaptable organizations. Leaders need to:

- do more than just provide people with secure jobs – they need to create environments that unleash their full potential.
- go beyond traditional offerings like fair pay and career development to create experiences that give people a sense of purpose, agency, belonging, and recognition.

Employee experience will be a crucial metric of business success for a long time. There will always be trends, especially ones that emerge from innovations in technology and communication. There will be black swan events, like the pandemic, that cause a bigger rethink than was imagined. There will be shifts in social norms that change the nature and demands of work. Once upon a time, size outpaced more than just about any other organizational asset, only to be replaced in recent years (thanks to Moore's Law and explosions in microprocessing) by speed and agility. As stated earlier, America's top CEOs touted "shareholder capitalism" repeatedly for a generation until they didn't, and it was time to replace it with "stakeholder capitalism." Still, it's hard to imagine a time when elevating worker experience will be deemed unimportant.

At this point, I hope you're no longer wondering *why* to build such a culture, but rather *how*. A study from Qualtrics XM Institute titled "Three Shifts for Employee Experience Success" encourages companies to alter their mindset in these ways:

1. from functional job execution to purpose-led empowerment
2. from disinterested surveying to collaborative understanding and action
3. from HR-driven programs to employee-engaging leaders[17]

Each organization will have its own formula for creating and improving employee experience. The chapters that follow will share instructive stories of good – and bad – employee experience, how management adapts, as well as insights into building a strong foundation centered on trust, purpose, and inspiration.

How can leaders, managers, CHROs, and others position their companies to thrive in the new world? Some questions they'll want to ask themselves:

- Is my view of the employee experience changing?
- How does my company need to change to improve the employee experience?
- How will we find the best people?
- What are the most effective ways to retain them?
- How will we solve for high performance simultaneously with high employee fulfillment?
- How can we inspire a culture where employees are encouraged to constantly reinvent themselves, and in doing so, reinvent their skill sets for the future?
- How can managers lead their teams in meaningful and effective ways?
- What has the pandemic revealed about people and connection?
- How can we improve productivity by putting people, rather than HR practices, at the center of the process?
- How can we develop a sustainable workforce, one that enjoys equal access to learning and skill development?

I talk to leaders and customers all the time, but my passion is employees, the backbone of success. Talking with our employees gives me insight into our business health, our customers, and the risks and opportunities in our future. I think about our business metrics all the time, but my focus is on employees. It's an ever-changing landscape, but the only way to drive growth and innovation and improvements in our business is to stay close to our people and our culture.

I'm not suggesting it's easy to change culture. I'm not suggesting we can even agree on what's happening in the world of work. I hear some people talk about the unique opportunities that exist right now, and job openings that exceed in number the people able or willing to fill them. Moments later, I hear people lamenting that they're working harder than ever, because their colleague left and there's no one to fill the gap, and they're told to "suck it up," doing more work for the same pay. Which has made them feel – bizarrely – simultaneously more valued *and* less valued. One worker we spoke to said she was of two minds about a dress code at her place of employment: "There are no uniforms here, so it's a more casual job, which is both a positive and negative," said Anna, manager at a food market. "Positive because you feel you can be more yourself, we all feel it, which leads to more camaraderie, and I have made so many good friends among my co-workers, which was so helpful during the pandemic when they were the only people I would see. But then the casualness made some people take the job less seriously than they should."

There is no one view or definition we can all agree on.

The other day, I asked my son, Cole, an 18-year-old member of the iGeneration and a future employee, "What is experience?"

"A great experience," he said, "is memorable and impactful. Whether it's negative or positive, you learn something from it. Oh, and other people are involved."

True, I'm biased, but I find that to be about as eloquent a description of the concept as I've come across. At its core, experience is about gaining knowledge, changing the way we understand and operate in the world around us. As I referenced earlier, a recent survey stated that the single biggest factor for determining whether people stayed with a company was the availability of opportunities for learning and development. We are fortunate that our knowledge economy allows so many with curiosity to educate themselves, to set themselves up for something better.

And there is some social element, an opportunity to engage with others.

When employees talk about setting themselves up for something better, there are many things to consider.

The Whole Self Model™
Who You Are and Who You Are Becoming

Photo Source: SAP SuccessFactors/Adobe Stock

The whole self framework is a lens into how employees experience change and opportunity throughout their careers. Each employee has a unique experience, the elements of which include work styles, mindsets, experiences, aspirations, passions, and more. These elements dynamically change just as we do.

In an ideal scenario, employees can align their whole self with their work. They feel a sense of hope, efficacy, resilience, and optimism. This sense of fulfillment is described as having high psychological capital; thus people become far more encouraged and motivated by their work: They can take on anything. When psychological capital is higher overall, it creates organizational durability in times of change.

When it comes to reskilling and upskilling, the whole self framework can be employed to help people autonomously seek out opportunities. In turn, they feel a far greater sense of connection to their organization because their work aligns closely with who they are and who they wish to become. They can navigate unpredictable circumstances but are also more likely to engage autonomously; think creatively; experiment with new ideas, roles, or opportunities; and evolve from paper pushers to mountain movers for their organizations.

Organizations can develop talent as well as create and access a rich set of data. Businesses can gain real-time insight into what inspires their people, to better understand what programs are effective and what skills are being developed across their workforce. Leaders will know how best to pivot their talent at a moment's notice, whom to bring on, and where to redeploy — all in a mutually beneficial way. For every opportunity an organization can provide, it will have a transformative effect on both the individual and the business.

This connects the dots: where an employee's whole self is fulfilled, psychological capital is high, and it spills over across teams and broader areas of the organization, at scale, to transform culture and drive better business outcomes.

We want work to be meaningful. Nurturing. Passion-satisfying. Joyful.

I sincerely believe that when employees find their purpose and passion, the strength within them that represents their unique value: That is when they experience joy at work.

What a concept! Who could have thought such a thing 3,000 years ago, or even 100?

The X Factor: A Belief in People

People are at the heart of everything. This isn't news. Our experience colors everything, in life and at work. Yet it feels a little strange to talk about fulfilling experience in the same breath as "work." For so long, the vast majority of business enterprises and their leaders made no real attempt to transform work and all that comes with it into something enjoyable and inspirational. For consumers, yes; partners, sure; shareholders, you bet; executives, absolutely.

Employees? Not so much. It's taken far too long for the worker to be properly valued, much less considered the linchpin to success. Who in business leadership or management considered their employees' work-life balance before, say, a generation ago?

At our core, we believe that human beings need engagement. We believe we deserve dignity and respect. We deserve opportunity and a path to betterment. We don't always achieve the ideal of having a superior human experience, but we at least chase it, for ourselves and those we care about. We aim to achieve it at home and in school, in our relationships, in our socializing. We try to enhance experience for our spouses and partners, children, parents, students, colleagues. *Experience* can hardly be teased out from what we do; in many ways it *is* what we do. It's all we do.

But let's be honest: It's often not, especially not in our work life. For far too many people and far too many companies, there's work . . . and then there's life. There's work . . . and then there's whatever isn't work. Where a gap exists between the two – where work feels like something apart from and less nourishing than life – how do we shrink it?

A requirement for building an employee-first culture is a belief in people. I know this from firsthand experience. All of us have skills, a unique set. But if people are put in defined, limited situations where they can't or don't thrive, they may just stay there, frustrated, joyless, far less productive than they could be, enduring a bad experience themselves and ill-equipped to provide positive ones for customers and/or fellow employees.

When I first landed in Singapore to take a new leadership position within SAP, a woman named Sarah, a part-time contract worker, gave me my badge and the keys to the office. Sarah had been hired as an office assistant, in charge of keeping my calendar and filing expenses. But I could right away see her superpower. She made me instantly comfortable in a foreign country. I was by myself – my husband and our two kids wouldn't arrive for another six months – and Sarah quickly became so much more than an executive assistant. She created a great experience for me.

One day, I told Sarah, "You know what? You're really good at creating a great experience for people. Why don't you plan our next quarterly meeting? That way, you're in charge of giving others what you've given me."

"But my job is to put things on your calendar," she said.

"I know that. But I'm asking you to challenge yourself. I can see you're good at a lot more than calendars."

I was not at all surprised that the rich agenda and experience Sarah prepared for our entire, diverse Asia Pacific and Japan team was extraordinary. Sarah quickly grew beyond the limited role she was hired for. She became a full-time employee and continued to deliver great experiences. Sarah found her purpose and joy at work.

I understand why, when highly paid consultants come in to evaluate a flailing company, they start with strategy. We know that strategy is key to growth. But here's the thing: While there are surely strategic shortcomings to address and correct, the focus probably should be on the talent already in the building, yet to be unleashed.

Looking internally at talent and how to unleash people's full potential is often far more valuable than creating an entirely new strategy. Many companies focus too much on creating strategies that *tell* employees what things to do instead of creating environments where employees are inspired and enabled to do what needs to get done.

It can be hard to see people as the best solution. In business, we're taught that everything that matters can be measured. And a focus on people sometimes seems difficult to measure.

That's not true – not anymore. Those of us in the business of measuring such things have proof that people are more than capital or assets. Employees who enjoy a positive, memorable experience help drive a company's vision. They drive positive business outcomes. They bring out the best in other employees (who are then also, presumably, having positive experiences). They connect their own passion to their company's purpose – which creates an experience that is authentic. Metrics consistently show that a fulfilling employee experience correlates with better health and well-being, higher engagement, and more willingness to take risks.[18] It also correlates to business success. The Thrive XM Index, built in partnership with Thrive Global, Qualtrics, and SAP SuccessFactors, takes a holistic view of employee well-being to examine the root causes of issues that affect employees and business. They found that the 20 companies that ranked highest with experience grew on average by 16 percent year over year.[19]

I believe in people. I believe in the individuals who come to work every day and strive to bring their best self. Sometimes they're not sure they're good enough. Or that they contribute adequate value. Or that what they have to offer is the right thing at the right time. I try to see in people what value they can bring, then maximize that, knowing that if I succeed, it's a force multiplier for the business. Sometimes you fit the job to the person, not the other way around. It's magic, but it's not. The "trick" is to engage employees in a world focused on independence and self-orientation; to promote the tackling of challenges with a sense of adventure; and to encourage employees to reinvent themselves, constantly. New skill sets better prepare them for the future, *their* future, no matter whom they're working for.

We've come a long way in the evolution of employee experience, and things are evolving faster than ever before.

Four things define a positive employee experience: Purpose, Agency, Belonging, Recognition.

The first and underlying "X Factor" in employee experience is a sincere belief in people.

Breaking Down Employee Experience

Your employees are your company's real competitive advantage. They're the ones making the magic happen – so long as their needs are being met.

Richard Branson

CHAPTER 3

More Than a Job

Purpose, Meaning, Connection

If your last name is Miller, then somewhere on your family tree you're very likely to find people who milled. If your name is Baker, there are bakers in your lineage. If you're a Butcher, you had butchers. If your name is Cooper, some of your ancestors made barrels.[1] You can draw a similar conclusion about the "occupational origins of surnames such as Archer, Barber, Bowman, Brewer, Butler, Carpenter, Carver, Cook, Draper, Farmer, Fisher, Forester, Fowler, Gardener, Hunter, Mason, Piper, Potter, Sadler, Sheppard, Shoemaker, Skinner, Tanner, Taylor, Weaver and Wheeler."[2] In Spanish and Portuguese, there's Chaves (maker of keys), Herrera (ironworker), Machado (maker of hatchets), and Zapatero (shoemaker). You get the point.

There was a time when the connection to one's job was literally inseparable from one's name. Who you were was what you did, and vice versa.

With every generation, the world, and the world of work, grows more "complex and specialized, with many of our emerging professions orienting around abstract products and services far removed from the historical tasks of our species (e.g., nanotechnology, mobile entertainment, and business applications)."[3] I haven't yet met someone with the last name CybersecurityGovernanceRiskAndComplianceLead, but maybe one day.

Once upon a time, theologians and philosophers validated work as a way of serving a greater purpose and greater good. John Calvin "affirmed the view that all legitimate areas of work possessed inherent dignity to the extent that they contributed to the common good, and argued that a person's station had to be judged according to its capacities as an instrument of direct or indirect social service."[4] This notion became a bedrock of Puritanical thought in England and the United States in the 17th century, and underpins how many of us, at least in the U.S., still view work – that it is meaningful and purposeful, and that it serves a need beyond one's self and immediate concerns.[5]

Working for an organization, especially a large, global, multi-tiered one, your individual reason and motivation for working can easily seem distant and abstract. The more that disconnect happens, the less likely you are to feel purpose and meaning – or passion – in your job. Without aligning yourself in some way with the organization's reason for being – its *why* – work can feel uninspiring, soul-sucking; it can feel like, well, work. Burnout is typically portrayed as a consequence of too much stress and responsibility, something that will ease once we reduce some burden. But couldn't work burnout also be the result of a lack of something – like, meaning and purpose? If you introduce these, wouldn't energy be restored? It's hard to "row together" with your fellow workers if you don't care about or even understand the direction you're headed. Is it a direction you support? Are the leaders even clear about what the company's mission is? Has the company lost its way – or never had one? Historically, many companies thought of culture in terms of slogans and statements about mission and values. But words alone do not create a culture. Employees now expect much more. They want the experiences they have at work to reflect cultural values they believe in.

There are lots of things that employees today want and increasingly expect. They do not want to be "qualified," "selected," or "onboarded." They want to discover opportunities, learn about possible roles, be welcomed into organizations, and get recognized for their contributions. This means filling roles based more on what candidates want and not just what companies need. More than half of adults say it's critical to work somewhere that aligns with their purpose and values.[6] Happiness is not necessarily the #1 goal. According to authors of a recent article in *Harvard Business Review*, "We have some 800,000 data points collected over 20 years telling us what people value at work. The responses, from both white- and blue-collar workers in a wide variety of industries, fall into four broad categories: value, purpose, certainty, and belonging."[7]

"I would like to find meaning in what I'm doing because I'm going to spend half my life working, right?" says Jianyu, who handles phone sales for a U.K.-based tech-for-good app. "So how I define work is very important. If you see work as something you do just to get paid, then that sounds dreadful. It's not something I look forward to. But if work is something you voluntarily and willingly dive into, and are able to make an impact, and still feed yourself – then that's almost artistic, being able to express what you believe and how you see the world and what you want it to be in the future. That's real work."

If an employee isn't feeling something as powerful as this, how can leaders help?

Making It Real

For an employee to feel purpose in their company, they really need to believe in two things:

- the company's purpose (which may also be described as the future and ongoing state of the company's business)
- their own daily contribution to realizing that purpose

The company vision is a colorful, tangible, clear description of the company's purpose, bringing it to life so that employees, as well as other stakeholders, understand it. There must be clear, consistent communication of the vision, repeatedly, as well as the strategy (repeatedly), which is what it takes to make the vision achievable. A leader should also communicate (repeatedly!) that it is the community of assembled employees who turn the vision into reality.

That's what CEOs can do.

In too many companies, the stated purpose is only part of the whole purpose, and workers catch on quickly. "The motivation behind my last company was supposed to be making things better for patients, but it turned out to be 'save money' with every transaction," says Colleen, in health care. "For so many of us who went into this field, we care about the progress we're making against a disease or helping an individual or making sure medications are cost-effective and that patients can pick them up, those kinds of things. Making patients' lives easier and providing them with education and ongoing resources. The company preached all these things. In the end, the decisions they make are first and last about finances and profit."

Jianyu had a similar experience, for an app that's supposed to help people and the planet. "The stated mission is to fight waste, to help global warming, all that sort of stuff, but once you get into the company, it became very clear it's more about the numbers, the sales you close."

Of course, employees understand that their paycheck and a viable business model both matter. And the importance of the size of the former changes with a person's life stage. "When I was in my first job, it was all about the mission," says James, age 24, a veteran of two jobs. "Doing something meaningful while trying something new, those two kind of go together. Later on, I feel like I'll care more about compensation, when I'm thinking about buying a house and settling down and having a family."

"Managers need to work much harder these days," says Frances Botha, head of Human Resources for SAP-Asia

Pacific Japan. "Because money is not everything. The insistence on purpose, belonging – that's a big shift. My colleagues have talked about it for years but now you can actually see it happening."

Finding purpose can be elusive if the employee is not in the proper frame of mind. Anaya, a former junior tennis star in south Asia who retired from athletics and became a lawyer, says, "I was going through that phase where you don't know what you want to do with your life, because the only thing you knew doesn't work anymore." At first, it didn't much matter what her new employer stood for.

Meaning can be found in many pursuits, from personal relationships, to being in nature, to achieving athletic or physical goals, to artistic expression, to charitable acts: We spend so many hours at work, we hope we can find it there, too. Especially there.

Connecting to the Why

At one point in the 1960s, as the United States and the Soviet Union raced to beat each other to space, several reporters visited NASA and came upon a janitor. One reporter asked the man, broom in hand, "So what is your job at NASA?"

"It's my job to help put a man on the moon," replied the janitor.[8]

Does the employee know why they are doing what they're doing? Can they connect the dots from their actions at work to the ultimate benefit they deliver? There are plenty of stakeholders inside the company who are beneficiaries of one's work. But I don't mean those people. If an employee is helping to produce a product or to provide a service, who is the ultimate beneficiary of that work? If you see yourself on one end of that chain, do you know who's all the way at the other end?

Twenty years ago, the prominent organizational psychologist Adam Grant conducted a field experiment, ostensibly to increase sales. The experiment examined the connection between the "seller" and the ultimate prospective consumer. In the study, college students at the University of Michigan cold-called alumni for donations, which would be used for new buildings, faculty and staff salaries, athletic teams, and scholarships. The students who volunteered were not all that invested in how well they did their job or their success rate. Then a scholarship student was invited to come speak to one group of callers. He spent a few minutes telling them that it was work like theirs that helped fund his scholarship and changed his life, and he wanted to thank them. Another group of callers did not meet the scholarship student. Over the next month, the first group of callers increased the time they spent on the phone by 142 percent and the money they raised by 171 percent; the other group showed no discernible change. Grant calls this "outsource inspiration": the spark comes from the ultimate beneficiary of the service or product, not from a leader exhorting people to work harder.[9]

Syad, an engineer, says, "in software development, connecting your why to the team why, and then the team's why to the next-level leader's why: It becomes a game of telephone, basically. At a certain point nobody knows what needs to be done, quite honestly. Why am I doing this? You end up losing the thread, the purpose. Sure, I wrote my two, three, four lines of code today, but I don't see who's consuming it, what that end customer looks like. There are so many functional silos within a company. Developers have struggled for a long time to understand what impact they're having on the bigger strategy."

To correct this disconnect, a few leaders in his company came to speak with the young developers and "articulated very clearly how something like this actually goes out. It was very welcome because we had never gotten that guidance, and our yearning to be connected to the larger why had been growing and growing." But even better – as per Grant's conclusion – one of the managers knew what would really help. "'You know what, guys?' he told us. 'I'm bringing in customers and we'll have a whole day of interactions with them.'" A variety of customers came through – "somebody was live on CRM software, somebody live on SRM, there were IT customers, the people who use our software every day. To be able to interact with them, and hear them tell us how they were using particular components and what it was doing for their company, the issues they were having. That was such an important moment for us, it gives me goosebumps even now."

How many levels separate the producers of products and providers of services from their final intended audience? If it's so many that you would need binoculars to see them, then that needs correcting.

Dr. Autumn Krauss, organizational psychologist and Chief Scientist at SAP SuccessFactors, recalls her experience researching the work culture at a diamond mine in Canada. The mine owner wanted to "close the gap" between the miners and those they were serving. "This is a place where generations of families had worked – dads and grandfathers, brothers had all worked there," says Autumn. "A lot of them are indigenous people who had worked in this mine that's basically underneath the ice year-round. Their job was moving earth, literally thousands of tons of dirt, and they'd never seen any of the diamonds that came out of the mine. We suggested they change some of their practices, including having tours of the diamond room for workers. It would also be part of the onboarding for new miners, so they would have an opportunity to see what they would be producing.

They went even further, to show the ultimate beneficiary – how the people who buy diamonds use it to celebrate special occasions, engagements, anniversaries, the birth of children. The workers could see that through moving all that earth, all day long, underground, they were helping to create unforgettable experiences for people."

I heard of a plastic extrusion plant that did the same thing: An employee suggested that the company create a display case showing products that the plastic was used for. When workers brought their kids in, the proud employee could say, "This is what your dad/mom helps to build." They talked about how their kids would be in the grocery store, point at a bottle of something, and say, "My dad made that!" – a bit more rewarding than saying, "My dad works in a chemical factory!"

At SAP, we naturally spend lots of time supporting our customers. Yet it's important for us to link to the true beneficiary of our work, a customer further down the chain – beyond the CTO, the CIO, the IT leader, or the CHRO. I mean those who benefit from our software – the recruiter, the learner, the rewards expert, the employee, the contractor. The better we get at identifying and recognizing the very end user – the person at the end of the last mile – the better our employees (researchers and designers and developers and support teams) are able to see the true result of their work, putting a face to something previously abstract. It humanizes their work. Whom are we ultimately trying to serve? Are they satisfied with our efforts? Can we meet some of them?

Leaders should strive to keep that line of sight in mind and help their team always to have it in mind, too. How much will it mean to those on the ground, at the lower levels in an organization, to be able to make that connection?

It gives a *why* to the *what*.

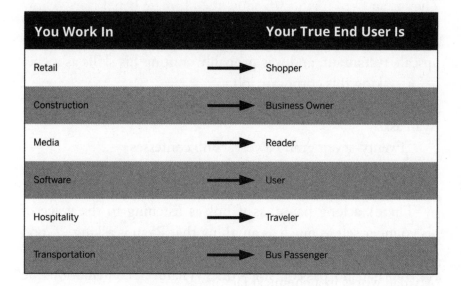

You Work In		Your True End User Is
Retail	➤	Shopper
Construction	➤	Business Owner
Media	➤	Reader
Software	➤	User
Hospitality	➤	Traveler
Transportation	➤	Bus Passenger

Passion Drives Purpose

In the movie *Up in the Air*, George Clooney's character, Ryan, is a corporate "downsizer" – a hired gun who flies from city to city, visiting company after company, firing employees so that the company's leadership doesn't have to. He's been at it for a long time so he knows the range of reactions to expect – deeply negative, of course, including rage, disbelief, sadness, hatred, hopelessness. With his soothing voice and unflappable manner, he does about as good a job as you could expect to "manage" people during one of the worst moments of their lives.

But he is not without humanity. At one point, after telling an employee named Bob (played by J.K. Simmons) that he is being let go, and listening to Bob vent about the horror show that awaits him and his family – no money to pay the mortgage, losing their home, no money for his daughter's medication, losing luster in the eyes of his kids – Ryan says that Bob's kids probably never admired him. Stunned and livid, Bob curses at Ryan until he hears Ryan's real point: that Bob once had bigger hopes than working his whole life for the faceless corporation he's now being let go from. Ryan can see from Bob's résumé that years ago in college he minored in French culinary arts, then worked at an upscale restaurant, and was probably crafting his skills as a chef before taking this corporate job.

"How much did they first pay you to give up on your dreams?" Ryan asks.

"Twenty-seven grand a year," Bob confesses.

"And when were you going to stop, and come back, and do what makes you happy?"

There's a long pause, as if Bob is listening to the voice of his younger self as much as anything that Ryan is asking. "Good question," says Bob.

Bob had no passion for work. Whatever contributions he made at his job, he did not feel connected to purpose. He had lost his way and lost his why.

There are so many legitimate, valid, excellent reasons for any-one to work where they do, even when doing something they're not passionate about. For lots of people, the rationalization got even more airtight during the pandemic and the widespread eco-nomic woes that followed.

Be grateful I have a job.

Bills need to be paid.

Who knows how long this will last?

Feel fortunate my job lets me work from home.

There are simply no better opportunities out there.

I don't have the skills/patience/connections/age/energy to find a better job.

I'm not suggesting that anyone quit their job. But a job no longer feels like one when you love it.

"I love science," says Yvette, a nurse specializing in kid-ney health, "and I also really like caring for people." When she learned about the specialty of nephrology, "I found it fascinating and loved having a particular subject to be an expert in. I really like knowing everything about one thing instead of a little bit about the whole body and every system."

Katherine, who dreamed of being in the film industry – and works in it now – says, "It seems like almost everyone genuinely cares about and is actually driven by the material they're making. It seems like an across-the-board belief that what they're doing is important. Maybe it's the highly collaborative nature of the business."

We all want that, not this: "They have me doing a lot of email marketing and blog posts, which I just hate," says Becca, a talented writer. "It feels like pieces of my soul are being sucked away."

Passion and joy are so important, yet they're often among the first aspects of life (in work and otherwise) that get sacrificed. When that happens, do we immediately do everything we can to restore these positive qualities to our lives? No. Meaningful work gets delayed, or ignored, and before you know it, you're Bob, sitting in front of someone asking you very candidly when you stopped caring.

Passion isn't just an emotional state that feels good. Passion is what you feel when you have purpose. When you work on something you're passionate about, you can achieve "flow." In flow, you are more productive, more efficient, and time flies. Employers can help employees find their state of flow, and both parties benefit.

One of the most profound jobs that leaders can do for employees is to create a system to help them connect to their passion, and thus find more joy. In her best-selling book *The Life-Changing Magic of Tidying Up*, Marie Kondo challenges readers to ask themselves if a particular possession sparks joy, and to get rid of those that don't. What if a manager helped their employee apply the same approach to work tasks and activities? It requires thoughtful consideration, because sometimes a task does not give you joy but accomplishing the task does. And there's an added benefit to this exercise: Evaluating daily tasks can surface those things that don't need to be done anymore at all – creating a better use of the employee's time and effort.

It is up to leaders to drive processes that connect people to purpose. These processes will drive greater employee engagement, higher retention rates, and better business outcomes. When I was in Japan, I learned the concept of *ikigai* and its four components: doing what you love, what you're good at, what you can get paid to do, and what serves a purpose in the community or world. That's a powerful combination. When an individual feels all of that, things flow. When things flow, the employee doesn't have to be reminded why they do what they do. They want to. They want to do it well. The why answers itself.

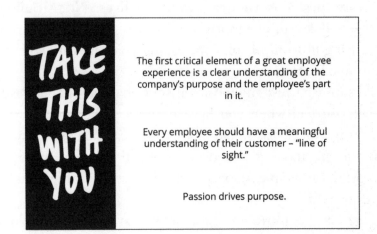

TAKE THIS WITH YOU

The first critical element of a great employee experience is a clear understanding of the company's purpose and the employee's part in it.

Every employee should have a meaningful understanding of their customer – "line of sight."

Passion drives purpose.

You Got This

Agency and Autonomy

We want to feel as if we're creating our own life – as if we have more than a little say in what it becomes and how we navigate the world. We want to feel as if we're getting better at the things that matter to us. We want freedom to use our strengths. We want to be the best version of ourselves.

These are universal truths, and they can't exclude who we are at work.

There is a reckoning within the workplace, accelerated by the pandemic, to reassess what work means. Employees are considering what they expect not only of their employer but of their job. How do they really want to work? Where do they want to work? What value do they get out of what they do at work?

It's not really up to organizations or leaders to answer these questions because no two individual employees will have the same answers. Employees need agency – the ownership and freedom to define what a great experience is for them – and autonomy – the permission to make it happen.

That means giving employees a significant say over crucial issues. Do they choose a hybrid, remote, or in-office setting? How will they pursue learning and growth opportunities? Where is their career going (whether it's ultimately with you or not)? It means helping them figure out the right answers for each of those questions.

The average length of time a person stays at one company is less than five years – and the number of careers a person has in their lifetime will only continue to grow. It's unrealistic to think that today's entry-level workers will follow the trajectory of past generations and remain with the same company until their retirement. This itinerant pattern isn't because of an unrealistic chase for the "dream job." It's the pattern of people evolving as individuals, pursuing different opportunities, and finding what fits – at any given time.

As I wrote earlier, defining the whole self means understanding who we are today and who we are becoming tomorrow. Most of what shapes who we are becoming falls outside the workplace, like starting a family, serving as caretaker for an aging parent, moving to a new place, or discovering a new passion. Each of these changes will impact how, where, when, and why we show up to work.

Agency and autonomy are the catalysts to ongoing growth.

Who Owns the Action?

"We've heard a lot about expectations around individualization, about employees growing accustomed to being catered to in their personal lives, through technology or social media, their very curated Amazon recommendations and Siri responses," says Dr. Autumn Krauss. "Marketing has got it all segmented down to a sample size of one. When we look at employee experience, we shouldn't be surprised that employees come to work wanting an individualized experience, specifically catered to them. Since they get advertisements aimed just at them, why wouldn't they want that to play out at work? Yet I spend time with some of the leading CHROs and no one is close to executing at that level, even where the data exist. They're just starting to get these wholesale experience strategies in place."

Yes, it's up to companies to create great employee experiences. But when they provide agency and autonomy, employees assume some of the responsibility to figure out what they need most. There is increasingly a move *away* from strategies pointing to the path to success and *toward* experiences that empower workers to create success in their own way. This trend shifts "towards a more human-centered interaction, empowering employees and encouraging responsibility."[1]

This doesn't mean leaders are off the hook. (In Chapter 7, I discuss the role of managers today and why they hold such an important role in this process.) Advocating for oneself is an acquired skill. Consider younger people entering the workplace for the first time. They may not know how they work best or learn best, and they most likely won't know what to ask for or whom to ask. Part of being a leader today is helping employees to identify their vision for where they want to be and take the steps to get there. This vision can be as lofty as a career aspiration 20 years from now ("I want to be the CEO"). In most cases, it will be a much more near-term goal, like building a new skill, finding a way to bring an underused talent to the team, or even trying out a different role to see if it's something to pursue more permanently.

Neville, a young architect, talks of the frustration at his previous firm, of wanting to do more than the assigned tasks, to show what he could do to make himself more indispensable. "Originally, I was hired to do certain things and, to their credit, they encouraged me to advocate for myself to join new projects, or even start up a project – yet it was unrealistic. With my amount of experience, it's difficult to do that when everyone is just too busy to give me guidance." He notes the unique dilemma of the mid-sized company: "When I was at a very small firm, with just a few principals, everyone had a personal connection with each other and I could ask for help and always get it because they knew me, and with so few people I was much more crucial, even if I was doing a lot of the grunt work. Now I'm at a very big firm with national standing, so there are enough people, senior or junior, that you can always find at least one person to help." With his previous firm, neither small nor big, such mentoring fell between the cracks. They took on more and more projects, so that they could increase their profile. But everyone was overworked, and no one had time to help him become more valuable. More than once, the senior person would take the shortsighted route and simply do a task that Neville had asked about, rather than taking the extra time to teach him.

Growth needs to be a shared vision between the employee and their manager in getting the employee to the best place.

"Every year we have salespeople assess themselves – for example, 'I am good at negotiation but not at C-level conversations,'" says one manager. "After that, your manager assesses you and then you look for gaps, especially where you think you're better than maybe you are. If you give yourself a five out of ten in one category and your manager gives you a two out of ten, then there's a significant gap. We use more data, filter it, then create a program that says, 'Here are your gaps, this is where we can help.' We're a backbone, ready for the employee to lean on if they need help. If they don't, that's entirely their choice."

Today's employees look differently at how they build their résumé. It is often less programmatic, less "climbing a traditional career hierarchy," says one HR person. "They bounce around."

"We see a big entrepreneurial spirit, a lot of them with 'side hustles,'" says another HR manager, of the trainees in her company's program. "They have that consciousness of the world, and it informs their creativity and inventiveness." She says her company "hired people, many of whom had their own businesses, mostly a part of Gen Z, and it's integrated into their core. We encountered a lot of 'I don't need you to teach me this information, I can find it, teach me what I don't know.' From Day One we relied heavily on role-playing and case studies. Every class was experiential learning, practicing things you could never just Google. We sell to 25 industries, so we had industry-specific classes for each and the students felt they were getting something valuable – a holistic, end-to-end picture of our solutions, our industry, our customer demographics, and the value of selling. There was heavy emphasis on human skills, a huge focus on customer empathy and getting in their shoes and learning."

Ideally, the stars will show themselves, through a combination of ambition, ability, and support. "I had a couple employees that went on to be managers," says one manager. "Not everyone has the skill set. But you want to open that path to them, give them as much support and teach them as much as you can. And with their initiative, and the things that they bring, they'll advance. That's what you hope for."

Learning, technology, and mentoring all play important roles in helping workers increase their viability, even if it means they may one day be starring elsewhere. Employees want a nurturing atmosphere and may be inclined to go where that's available. "In the oil and gas industry," says Todd, "I was basically responsible for my own destiny. They said, 'If you want to get new certifications, go to school, whatever, do it, but that's on you. We're not paying for any of it.' I took it upon myself to do it and it helped me get where I am today" – with a construction company that, in the last five years, "has been very good about promoting my accomplishments." Todd signed up for classes and "the company paid for everything."

As with parenting or investing, it's a tough balance between an involved approach or one that's more hands-off. The right balance and environment will ultimately come down to what will be most helpful to each individual – but getting this right can win the smart company the skills, leadership, and loyalty of great employees. Development, learning, and mobility should be honored. Leaders are rewarded for making their numbers. They should be equally rewarded for developing and retaining top talent and finding the right fit for people and roles.

A good friend once told me, "Never underestimate a person who was poorly led." It might sound depressing but it's actually full of hope. It makes me look at people who aren't doing a very good job as possibly being far more capable, even great, but who have been led poorly or not at all – by a bad or absent manager, a dumb system, a tense and unsupportive company culture, who knows what. That one statement has made me pause before judging people harshly. I look at those within my own organization, people who are clearly not shining or engaged or joyful, as possessing amazing abilities yet untapped. But they were poorly led. They were overstructured. Or they weren't given enough structure to show what they could deliver. Or they put up with a host of other crimes routinely committed against eager, talented, but misplaced workers.

For such employees, achieving autonomy is obviously harder, because often they themselves don't believe they're capable of success – and those around them almost certainly don't, since they've seen little evidence of remarkable contribution.

"I fell through the cracks, and I was always an afterthought," says Leila, whose manager-mentor was distracted and indifferent, not giving her a chance to shine and not providing meaningful feedback (sometimes none at all) on assignments she did carry out. "And I came from HR! I was doing organizational design and development and constantly waiting for leadership to bump my manager to a different role, get me access to someone else, or I had to come up with my own ways to find my own happiness." Though the last option seemed to give her the most control, it also didn't, because she had no one championing her. What's more, she resented doing it all on her own. "You spend at least 40 hours a week with people at work and I think they should have cared about my development and future."

To her credit, she tried to be proactive and remain positive, and it paid off. "Luckily, the role came along." That's the good news. The not so good? "It came along two and a half years later."

The world is full of individuals with great skills, original ideas, unbeatable work ethic, unique talents – all yet to be completely realized. Maybe they need to be in a different role, or on a different project, or in a different field altogether. Without a great mentor or champion, it may be harder or take longer for them to shine.

It's About Trust

"I like our CEO so much because soon after I got here, he brought me in for a meeting and said, 'Hey, a year from now, this is where I'd love to see you,'" says Rodney. "It wasn't necessarily a position change he was talking about – maybe, maybe not. It was more, 'This is the growth I want to see.'"

You can't have agency and autonomy without trust. Rodney was given direction, but he had the autonomy to determine how to meet the expectations set out. At the same time, the CEO had to trust that Rodney possessed the skills and determination to get there. Relationships are always based on trust.

Trustworthiness can be broken down into an equation – the Trust Quotient developed by Charles M. Green. First, we have to consider Credibility (if the person is believable), Reliability (if the person is dependable), Intimacy (if we feel safe sharing information with the person). Take all of that and divide it by Self-orientation – how much the person is focused on oneself.

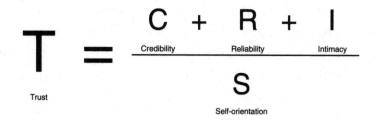

$$T = \frac{C + R + I}{S}$$

If leaders can reduce their self-orientation and put employees at the center of the conversation, with a focus on their growth and development, trust increases. And with a foundation of trust, people feel more empowered to take chances and even fail. Strong cultures of innovation and growth are built on this foundation.

"I was doing well, contributing well, not thinking about the next step when someone approached me with an opportunity in field readiness," says Bella. "I hadn't heard of it before. I had no idea what it meant. But I trusted myself. I asked myself if I could handle the worst scenario, which I figured in this case would be that I fail. The answer was yes. I ended up getting the job and I've been in the role for four years."

Trust is essential not only for relationships. It's fundamental to inspiring employees. Trust makes it possible for employees to believe in the vision for the company, the leaders that are steering the ship, and their own capabilities to power the change, innovation, and creativity needed for continued growth.

It's About Choice

As humans, we crave the ability to create an environment that is safe and familiar. We want the control to create our own destiny. Richard Branson, CEO of Virgin Enterprises, said, "Choice empowers people and makes for a more content workforce." By providing employees with choice, it allows them to control aspects of their work, whether it's their physical environment or the manner in which they complete a project or task. Research shows that in jobs with high stress, employees who have more autonomy in dealing with that stress and decision-making tend to experience (it won't surprise you) significantly less stress.

Most employees crave a workable combination of structure and freedom: the former so that everyone is clear on their responsibility, the latter so that their individuality can shine through.

Having choices clearly benefits the employee. It's also a necessity for the business. As much as we'd like it, we can't predict the skills or requirements that business will need in the future. Choice triggers curiosity. Curiosity leads to adaptability. And adaptability is the not-so-secret sauce to ongoing success in our ever-changing world of technology and ideas.

The added step beyond providing choice is ensuring that employees can discover and pursue opportunities. To this end, internal talent mobility will become a differentiator for organizations as they continue to face fierce competition for talent and address an ongoing skills gap. Many organizations are already beginning to implement internal talent marketplaces where employees can find short-term projects, fellowships, mentors, networking, learning activities, and more.

The LinkedIn Workplace Learning 2021 report found that "employees at companies with internal mobility stay almost two times longer" and "employees who move into new jobs internally are more than three times more likely to be engaged employees than those who stay in their current jobs."[2]

The choice provided by internal talent mobility is key to unlocking potential. HR industry analyst Josh Bersin describes the talent marketplace as "the next form of business management. It will facilitate the evolution from the hierarchical model where you work your way up the pyramid to being an agile, creative, resilient organization where people work on multiple projects, move from role to role and embrace job sharing."[3]

Helping people find the right opportunities and giving them freedom to explore and pursue these possibilities empowers them to try new things and see what works. Choice creates a sense of flexibility and possibility so that employees are moved to stay.

"The opportunity to move around and grow my skills is clearly there," says one developer who has recently been considering a more managerial role. "Whether I take advantage of those positions or just decide that I want to continue in this role is up to me, but I like that there are opportunities within my company that I could pursue."

That's not the only way in which it's the employees' world and we must accommodate it. If the current situation is not satisfying for an employee, then they may look to "job craft – changing [their] job to make it more engaging and meaningful."[4] Any job, according to Jane E. Dutton and Amy Wrzesniewski in their article in *Harvard Business Review*, can be broken down to the various traits that make it what it is: "Task crafting . . . involves altering the type, scope, sequence, and number of tasks that make up your job. Next, you can relationally craft your job by altering whom you interact with in your work. Finally, there is cognitive crafting, where you modify the way you interpret the tasks and/or work you're doing."[5] When companies invest in dynamic measures of skill qualification, they broaden the pool of skilled candidates they're looking at. Having x years of traditional schooling may not matter, and it certainly won't be the first or final measure of whether the worker is competent and capable.

Such training opens up an organization to an array of previously ignored employees (full-time, part-time, gig), and who's to say they're not your future? At a Human Resources conference I attended in 2019, a CHRO of a large beverage company in Central America recounted how rolling out learning had an effect on hundreds of workers across Latin America who had lacked the opportunity to go to college. The CHRO saw their learning usage trend up on the weekend because these workers were so excited to learn from their cell phones, opening a new world. Her company provided learning content. The workers could access it easily. I find it moving that a person who's out selling pallets of sodas and chips comes home after a long day and thinks, "I can learn something new today."

In the age of remote and hybrid work, there is also more choice when it comes to location. In the past, a city or state government tried to recruit a company for the jobs it would bring to the new location and the revenue from all those relocated workers. Today, a relocated company may be of little economic value if employees are not going to the office. To adjust to this new reality, writes Brian Kopp, "states and cities will start to use their tax policies to create incentives for individuals to relocate to their jurisdictions rather than giving tax credits solely to large companies to relocate." Topeka, Kansas, and Tulsa, Oklahoma, for example, are offering remote employees up to $15,000 to move to their city.[6] More than 20 countries – including most of the Caribbean – now offer remote work visas.[7] Others go even further, paying you to relocate – among them, Vietnam, Denmark, Greece, and New Zealand.[8]

Simply put, employees today have choice. They're not motivated solely by money but also by culture, purpose, learning, and flexibility. Choice is a competitive differentiator. If every employee has different needs for a good experience, and also craves greater autonomy, then it stands that the approach to each employee must differ. One-size-fits-all was a problematic idea to begin with, but in today's world of better employee experience it's not just inadequate. It's the very opposite of a smart employee experience approach. Resources need to match the worker.

What Next?

Agency and autonomy are not just about bigger titles, personal advancement, and greater compensation. They're about the desire for more responsibility so that employees can have a greater impact, thus more control over what they're putting out into the world. "If you don't feel control and you're not able to change that fact, then how do you really make that impact?" says one employee. It's great to want to make a difference, but there needs to be a platform for it.

When work feels limiting in this way, employees get frustrated. They feel disengaged. Those skilled and fortunate enough to be able to consider alternatives, short or longer-term, start to wonder: Is there more than this? Am I better off living a different life? Are parts of me being ignored? What would it be like if I felt like I was living my potential? Am I better off at another firm?

By providing agency and autonomy for employees to shape their career in alignment with company goals, workers are more likely to feel ownership in the company's growth. They will be more engaged, empowered, and indispensable, because they're on an upward trajectory. And they will fight harder to help the company win, because people are more likely to support that which they have had a hand building. If they feel like they are on a path of their choosing, in a domain that aligns with their values and passions, and with a purpose that fulfills their needs, they will work hard to deliver on the mission.

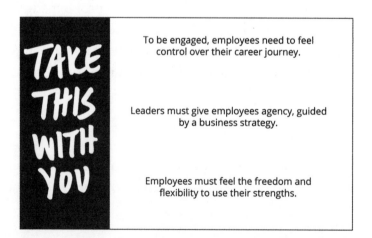

TAKE THIS WITH YOU

To be engaged, employees need to feel control over their career journey.

Leaders must give employees agency, guided by a business strategy.

Employees must feel the freedom and flexibility to use their strengths.

We Belong

Progress on Diversity, Equity,
and Inclusion

It's fairly easy for us to see where bias issues are throughout the organization but not in recruitment – in recruitment it's hard. Not everyone has massive recruitment data. It would be so data-heavy to record every single interview, every piece of feedback, etc. And unless you have that data, you can't tell that in this department, say, this manager hasn't put any non-males, non-Koreans, etc., through to the second round interview. We need the data.

—HR Officer at Global Corporation #1

In our short list for final consideration there are 3–5 candidates. But what percentage of the time is there a woman or underrepresented minority in that final slate? How many times does that convert to a hire? Would love to do more analysis on the front end. Also, different locations – different outcomes?

—HR Officer at Global Corporation #2

We want to take a stronger data-driven approach. We want to start capturing information about applications, how many do we get, how many are women, how many women pass screening, how many women get selected, how many get promoted, how many turn over? We're trying to get a better understanding of what is currently driving the current state.

—HR Officer at Global Corporation #3

We're past the point of debating the virtues – both societal and business – of more diverse, equitable, inclusive workplaces. But because of a lack of discernible progress in many companies, they're worth repeating. Diverse workplaces attract individuals from a broader pool, thus providing greater insights and creativity. Teams working in an inclusive culture outperform their competition by an extraordinary 80 percent.[1] Inclusive businesses generate more revenue and way more cashflow per employee.[2]

It's especially important now, as so many businesses have either been moved from within or pressured from without to address diversity, equity, and inclusion (DE&I). The world is different today from five years ago. Customers are interested in different things, as are employees and the public at large. Employees aren't looking for a neutral stance – they're now putting pressure on their organizations to *do* something. Workers expect employers to combat issues and enact broader, societal change. They want to work for a company that does good for the world.

Priorities have shifted. What was once looked at as a "like-to-have" has now become an imperative. Organizations are being forced to "walk the talk" when addressing social justice issues and creating a workplace where all employees, regardless of identity, can thrive.

Yet as one colleague describes it, "I was at a conference and someone gets up there to talk about tangible actions to progress DE&I, and I've got my notepad out. And after a few minutes I thought: *What am I going to write down? You're not saying anything.*"

To bring DE&I to action, we have to start with belonging. Research by Coqual, a global, nonprofit thinktank and advisory group with expertise in DE&I, indicates that "someone belongs at work when they are seen for their unique contributions, connected to their coworkers, supported in their daily work and career development, and proud of their organization's values and purpose."[3] Businesses that foster a strong sense of belonging – where workers can bring their whole, authentic selves – win. (This invokes the whole self model I discussed in Chapter 2.)

Maslow's hierarchy reflects this: Belonging is the next most essential need above basics like food, shelter, and safety. Humans crave connection. We physically need it. Connection lowers our anxiety and reduces depression, helps us regulate emotions, raises self-esteem and empathy, and even boosts our immune system. Connection also influences how we remember and learn.

The same goes for the workplace. By creating opportunities for social connection, leaders promote a sense of belonging at work.

So: more happy hours? Not exactly.

EY's Belonging Barometer study examined how 1,000+ American adults define belonging – what makes them feel as if they belong or excluded in the workplace. They found that "more people get that sense of belonging from their jobs than any other source, outside of their own homes." It's about finding a space where people feel trusted, respected, valued, and have the ability to speak freely and voice their opinion. Leaders can create this with small steps every day.

It starts by bringing the right people together, in the right ways. Leaders should consider who they're inviting to meetings. Do those around the table have a diverse set of backgrounds and perspectives to solve problems? Does each person have a clear role and purpose? Is the leader encouraging input from all attendees?

Once employees feel they're contributing and adding value, they begin to build intentional connections with their peers, leaders, and organizations. This sense of purpose promotes belonging in the workplace. Employees will feel free to bring not only their ideas but their preferences, motivations, and aspirations.

Bringing your whole self to work doesn't come without risk. There's potential disappointment, rejection, hurt – or worse, discrimination. And the risk isn't felt equally, either. It may not be as easy for members of certain groups who have long been told *not* to bring their whole selves or were asked to hide parts of themselves. How do we create a workplace free of judgment, where contribution speaks the loudest?

Truth 1: Behavior change is hard.

Truth 2: Bias is often unconscious.

Conclusion: Removing bias from one's behavior will not happen without real effort.

By bringing quantitative data to our qualitative assumptions, we begin to uncover where we're stuck today. Technology facilitates those discoveries by highlighting individual blind spots, identifying and remediating structural problems, and innovating new ways to address them systematically.

Business Beyond Bias

Amanda Rajkumar, Adidas's Executive Board member responsible for Global Human Resources, has said with great candor, "Pretty much every company I've worked with has an unconscious bias training program, but has no evidence whatsoever on whether it's working or leading to any meaningful behavior change, let alone real progress for women and people of color into leadership roles."[4]

Businesses have to adopt a growth mindset when it comes to DE&I. It isn't something we'll ever "fix." It doesn't have a finish line. To effect sustainable change, we have to move away from solving for a single issue. The foundation of bias is deep and it will require processes that evolve every day as we become more aware. Solutions will be an agile, adaptive set of discoveries and remediations. We all need to become more flexible and open.

Efforts until now have often been halting. 71 percent of organizations try to foster diversity and inclusion, yet a mere 11 percent claim to have such an environment today.[5] Not even one in four organizations hold their CEOs accountable for building a diverse and inclusive environment; "leadership often delegates this work to a director within HR."[6] Some of the biggest tech companies in the world – the biggest companies, period – have received extensive coverage for their lack of workforce diversity.[7] And there are organizations out there, frankly, that seem simply not to care about this, or even know the point of pursuing a DE&I strategy. Best-selling author and motivational speaker Simon Sinek says, "Very, very few . . . organizations know why they do what they do. And by 'why' I don't mean 'to make a profit.'. . . I mean: What's your purpose? What's your cause? What's your belief? Why does your organization exist?"[8] If that's true, then how can an organization come up with a smart strategy, a strategy with purpose, vision – and, yes, a sustainable profit motive?

Most leaders want to do something good for their company and for the larger world.

If the focus is just on the effort at DE&I rather than the business results it produces, the enterprise will falter. Companies concerned about public perception struggle over whether they even want a business decision to be seen as DE&I-focused or not. Some think that adding extra fields in a pull-down menu on their intranet to allow an employee to change his/her/their pronouns will move the needle. Alone, it won't. What *will* advance things is creating psychological safety and a culture of belonging that attracts, engages, and retains a diverse talent pool.

To thrive, companies need to be places where diverse talent can contribute to their full potential. Employees are what make them or break them. The broader the net the company casts to find talent to attract, including those whose potential has for too long gone unfactored, with their different backgrounds and perspectives underappreciated, the more the company thrives.

Many companies focus on unconscious bias training. As Adidas's Rajkumar notes, though, it's a widespread effort that comes with little evidence of meaningfully positive results.

How do you mitigate for this bias? If it's hard to "train it out" of a person, then how else can we address it? That's where technology can come in. With data and analytics, leaders can identify trends and recognize patterns, then use that information to influence how they make changes.

Leaders regularly convene to discuss who's up for promotion, who's rated for one bucket (e.g., high performer) or another (needs a development opportunity). A calibration tool makes the vetting logistically simpler and less administratively taxing. Now, what if rules and conditions were embedded in this tool so that an in-session bias alert flags something notable? For example, take Amy, a Black contributor. Amy's been put in the high performer bucket three years running, yet she's still not up for promotion. Why? What does that mean? The executives making the final recommendations may or may not realize this; if they were to see that it's not just Amy who's in this position but a statistically significant segment of workers of color – high performers being promoted at a substantially lower rate than their white counterparts – then they would need to address that. A tool that mitigates for bias would flag it, or perhaps flag that other candidates were underrepresented for their gender, sexual orientation, religion, ableness, and so on. "It would essentially say, 'Hey, manager, do you want to take a look at this? It seems a bit off,'" says an HR employee working on this effort for us. This helps mitigate what Daniel Kahneman calls our "System 1" thinking – that our decision-making isn't always conscious or rational but rather unconscious, biased, and based on intuition.[9]

While such a fix may seem elementary, if thresholds were embedded throughout, it could help paint a picture of what's going on. Crucially, it would do so not after the fact, merely providing a static corporate profile (see the quotations by HR officers at the start of this chapter), but actively, in the midst of important HR processes such as recruiting, hiring, promoting, and retaining. Embedded insights can take the form of language choice, or a promotion or reward distribution. The closer you track the insight to the source of the bias, the better. This helps elevate understanding and growth for individuals, moving from an abstract discussion to an opportunity for curiosity and ultimately behavior change.

There are challenges with this, naturally. Organizations will grapple with the paradox of wanting to understand, support, and promote their diverse workforce, on one hand, while respecting employee privacy and abiding by region-specific legislation on the other.

In 2016, SAP SuccessFactors began embedding DE&I principles in our talent software. We call this Business Beyond Bias. The mandate is simple: Use these tools and, among other benefits, you can identify and mitigate bias. To be honest, it went slowly at first. With the urgency of an even more aware world, we are now progressing.

Some people believe it's more about optics than improving the company's day-to-day business results. I disagree. Rajkumar puts it well: "We're not lowering the bar," she said, "we're widening the gate."[10] This is not a case of *I was qualified but didn't get the job because I don't fit the diversity mandates*. It's about winning companies, in a world growing more global and diverse by the hour, broadening their employee base and reaping the rewards of fresh, different talent and perspective.

It's not just about looking good to the world. It's about growth and innovation.

Democratizing Opportunity

Many DE&I efforts focus on recruitment and hiring, without sufficient follow-up. "Companies often think, 'Done, on to the next,' and no one's really addressing DE&I across the employee life cycle," says Dr. Lauren Bidwell, Decision-Making Psychologist & Product Strategy Researcher at SAP SuccessFactors. "We've seen an interesting shift in organizations that used to focus almost exclusively on hiring. What happens the rest of the employee life cycle? Some companies have employees from underrepresented groups leaving at a disproportionate rate. If you track that, why is it happening? Often, they're not getting the same development opportunities. Or they're not being selected for high-visibility projects. They're still underpaid. These are pieces that have been neglected and can no longer be ignored."

Companies can't just focus on recruiting and expect that to solve their issues. They are better served taking a systems approach: thinking across the entire employee life cycle and trying (a) to remove bias, and (b) to incorporate inclusion into the revamped system. The heart of DE&I in business is to create and democratize opportunities across the workforce, so that it's not always the same people, or the same types of people, being picked for high-visibility opportunities.

Take this example: A well-intentioned, fast-growing startup wanted quickly to create career paths for their high-performing, eager-to-advance employees. They introduced a self-nomination promotion process. Every six months employees had the opportunity to submit a write-up outlining what they had achieved and why they were ready for their next step. The application would be reviewed by a closed-door committee and a decision would be made within a few weeks. Sounds quick, easy, and fair, right?

Consider the profile of someone who would openly and freely self-nominate. After a year of the new promotion process, the company realized that they'd promoted a fairly cookie-cutter profile. Their process was riddled with bias.

So they opened up the promotion process beyond self-nomination to peer and manager nominations. Within six months they witnessed a dramatic difference in both applications and selections. Sometimes it can really be that simple.

In evaluating how things have been in the past and how they could be done better in the future, one of our clients recently used a climbing analogy. For the longest time, we've thought about professional success in terms of a ladder. You climb the ladder, and climb, and climb, a pretty straight shot to the upper rungs, maybe even to the top.

Do x, then y, then z. Achieve level a, then b, then c.

Now, perhaps we're better off thinking not of a ladder but a rock wall. There are numerous paths to the top. In a new world, this is true for everyone, not just those in underrepresented groups. There is a persistent, minority-specific problem, though: Is there anyone on that rock wall who looks like you?[11]

We need to evolve how we think about career growth. We need to think differently about talent assessment and capability. How do companies surface hidden talent? How do they evaluate potential? Do they develop more of a market-based approach balancing demand and supply of skills and capabilities? There are extraordinarily capable, talented people in just about every organization who aren't in the right roles, and who would be phenomenal in a role that they – or the company – currently doesn't envision.

Executing on all that I'm suggesting won't be easy. Some major mindset shifts and incentive structures have to happen. It's so transformative, it's central to the business. It's a leadership topic and a culture topic. It affects every department in the company.

But this is thinking beyond bias *concretely* – not just hoping for good outcomes.

Leaders should take a look at their company's entire employee life cycle and current practices. They should do this with a diverse group. Were these practices – from recruiting to learning to succession to compensation and more – designed with DE&I

in mind? It could be that the processes themselves created an uneven playing field. That might not have been the intention when they were developed, but processes don't get changed often. They remain in place for a long time, until something is very broken. We tend to leave things alone but for surface-level fixes.

A willingness to look at the root of their business practices is something that few organizations are doing, for many reasons. It can be extremely arduous, complex, costly, time-intensive. But if companies genuinely wish to establish greater accountability on DE&I, then some of their systems may need evaluating and major overhauls. Some companies are starting to create accountability mechanisms, such as tying leader pay and other rewards to DE&I measures such as employee engagement, talent mobility, or inclusion indexes.

Some companies are leveraging data and analytics so that managers can see the inflow and outflow of their talent. It also allows the company to project what Manager X's team is going to look like in five years if they continue with their current hiring and promotion approach. The company head may see that Manager X has a pattern of hiring only males, for instance. That's worth a conversation.

With greater accountability come greater sensitivity, thoughtfulness, and real change.

We also need to move away from the fiction of the "perfect candidate." For a long time, many leaders have had a notion of what they need in a prospective employee, a laundry list of particular skills. What about the candidate who does not have all that but possesses a world of potential? How do we actually assess potential? Should we start looking at potential differently? Do we have unconscious bias when we assess potential, or what we think of as the lack of polished readiness? Imagine if we could craft a way to assess potential for doing a job, a way that had nothing to do with where the candidate went to school, where they grew up, or even the skills they currently have. How much talent is being overlooked because we haven't yet worked out that formula?

More Than Lip Service

For years, in many places around the globe, there has been little more than lip service given to formal DE&I initiatives. Now, there seems to be a sea change, a real willingness to speak up and to listen. "It's not a daily topic like it is in the U.S.," one overseas company leader told us, "but no longer do we have to create awareness of the topic in each country."[12] Another business leader said, "In Spain five years ago DE&I didn't 'exist,' not as a mindset. Now every company here is very focused on this."[13] In Portugal, laws mandate that organizations must recruit a certain percentage of workers who identify as having a disability.[14] In Denmark, it is required to report gender equality.[15] Gender pay analysis may soon become mandatory for all European countries.[16]

Some efforts are hampered by laws that vary for different underrepresented minorities. "Right now for our DE&I efforts, data is available if an applicant discloses it," says another company head. "I can't tell you where people are falling out in terms of gender and minority. If I did, I'd know where to attack."[17]

Many organizations, because of legal mandates, can't force applicants to share information about race, ethnicity, sexual identity, age, or several other indicators. Some have created "Get counted" campaigns, particularly for the LGBTQ+ community, around camaraderie and transparency, and why sharing the data will ultimately benefit the employee. In short, *We as an organization are going to share with you who gets access to this data, why we need it, what the benefit looks like to you.* But there needs to be more transparency about how it will be used. It's no wonder that employees don't actively and excitedly fill out this information. Who can view it? Will it be tied to decisions? Companies need to do a better job of thinking through these elements and not expecting that employees will just hand over very private, personal data without knowing exactly what happens with it. There's a fear of negative repercussion. It's up to organizations to change the script.

In the United States, we can ask people to provide information related to their gender, and track the data; we cannot do it for race and ethnicity. Even if we could, how would we ultimately define ethnicity? How does a global company "operationalize" race and ethnicity in the U.S. versus Brazil, where Black means something very different? It becomes convoluted fairly quickly. It's difficult to create interventions or programs targeted at increasing x when you can't track x or even possibly define x.

Legal mandates can help to hold organizations accountable. In Europe, for example, pay equity mandates take the onus off of companies: They have to follow them. Addressing inequity requires a fluid, continuously evolving approach. Political policy, economic trends, and societal changes happen every day. If new legal mandates are coming, then you have to be ready. Company leaders don't want to be racing to catch up, scrambling to make sure their organization is not sued or penalized.

We've seen organizations in the U.S. take a proactive approach by opting for total transparency when it comes to things like pay, performance, and promotions. This helps limit bias, uncover favoritism, and instill a sense of accountability, for both the employee and the organization. It alleviates anxiety and insecurity and promotes a culture of trust among peers. When you're more transparent as a company, your people may feel more comfortable being transparent themselves.

At some point in the book-writing process, I turned to my son, Cole, for the view of a high school student. I asked for his definition of diversity and inclusion, from the perspective of an emerging employee. Again, I got a terrifically thoughtful answer. "Inclusiveness is being kind enough to listen and truly understand another person's stance, without judging or rushing to make your own stance known."

I had never thought of it like that, and it led me to two realizations:

1. So much of what I have been trying to say about DE&I centers around *intention*.

2. The key to being a great leader or team member is to be *less self-oriented*.

"Lip service" means thinking about a problem and "acting on it" ineffectively, cosmetically – considering first how it will make *you* look. If we can willfully step back from our own orientation and consider the stance of others, especially those we haven't fully and fairly and consciously considered before, we'll be better positioned to understand how our business can and will be improved.

Acknowledging that something needs fixing, then truly doing something about it: That builds credibility, trust, and respect. People hear about it. They want to work at a place like that.

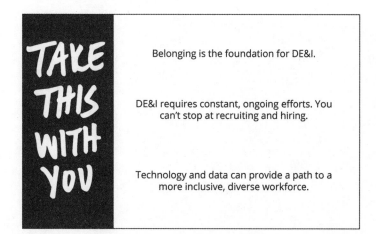

TAKE THIS WITH YOU

Belonging is the foundation for DE&I.

DE&I requires constant, ongoing efforts. You can't stop at recruiting and hiring.

Technology and data can provide a path to a more inclusive, diverse workforce.

I Value You

Belief, Recognition, Appreciation

When I think of the most inspirational leaders, talent developers, productivity drivers, people capable of creating a sustainable future for organizations, the name that comes to mind is not Warren Buffett. It's not Bill Gates. It's not Sheryl Sandberg or Peter Drucker.

It's Ted Lasso.

The fictional character, played by Jason Sudeikis in the Apple TV+ show of the same name, is an American championship college football coach whose social media-fueled exuberance leads him to be hired by the English owner of a Premier League team to coach soccer, a sport he knows almost nothing about. But Ted is a beacon in a world where cynicism, wariness, and self-involvement threaten to dull his light. He doesn't know the intricacies (and barely even the rules) of his new sport, but he does know about people and how to see each and every person as valuable in their own right. By doing so, he brings together the men in his charge as a genuine team, playing together and supporting each other in a way that makes them successful, and that is deeply satisfying and inspiring to their end users: the fans.

It is no surprise that the show struck a nerve, winning a slew of Emmy Awards, and becoming must-see TV even among people who neither know nor care about soccer. It's an oasis of upbeat in a sea of dystopian and escapist dramas. The world needs a major dose of Ted Lasso. Ted appreciates everyone around him, and tells them so. Often. Even those who seem not to respect him. He expresses his gratitude with equal fervor whether it's the towel boy or the owner of the team.

"I believe in hope," he says. "I believe in 'Believe.'"

"Please do me this favor, will you?" he tells his team after a devastating loss. "Lift your heads up and look around this locker room. Look at everybody else in here. And I want you to be grateful you're going through this sad moment with all these other folks because, I promise you, there is something worse out there than being sad. And that is being alone and being sad. Ain't no one in this room alone."[1]

In an interview, Sudeikis described his character this way: "Ted is egoless. He allows for people to be themselves and reflect what they think he is, but really what they are."[2]

What Ted Lasso is, more than anything, is transformative.

Many business leaders would do well to heed Ted Lasso's lessons. "For me, success is not about the wins and losses," he says. "It's about helping these young fellas be the best versions of themselves on and off the field."

Hold on there. Wait just one second. Why would I think a quotation about not caring about extrinsic success (wins and losses) would be at all instructional for CEOs and other leaders? Bringing out the best in people is all good and well, sure. But in a results-driven arena like business (and to be honest, Premier League soccer), saying that it's "not about the wins and losses" seems kinda . . . crazy?

Except that it's anything but. A positive culture yields success, optimal performance, minimal burnout. That kind of spirit helps to attract new talent, retain talent, and foster loyalty. In a landscape of increased remote work, fragmented work lives, stress, and self-questioning, conveying who you are as a company and what you value is grounding, both to prospective and current employees. There's nothing soft about leaders cultivating a nurturing, supportive ethos to help employees navigate the complexities they face at work, and in their personal lives, on a daily basis.

Belief, recognition, and appreciation are the fuel that keeps your company growing.

Everyone Has Value

I have so many people on my team who have so much capacity for incredible performance, yet there are days when they just don't believe it. Is it because they're not being properly valued? I would hope not. I want – as any leader would want – for all my people to feel valued all the time. I want them constantly to believe in themselves, so they'll be more willing to push themselves to do things they may even fail at, which I encourage. Every great learning moment in my own life has been one where I genuinely didn't know if I was about to fail.

It's up to leaders to bring out the value in their people, so that no individual or accomplishment gets overlooked. To do this, there needs to be genuine belief in the capabilities and skills that exist within all employees, including and maybe even starting with the most junior staff. In a world that has endured a pandemic, it might sound trite to say that everyone ought to be valued for their contribution. It's worth repeating.

"Some of the higher-ups who visited all the schools in the district made a point to know your name," says Janet, an elementary school teacher in the Southwest for more than 30 years. "It didn't matter who you were – the custodian, the bus driver, a teacher. When someone with clout who doesn't see you that often can call you by name, it makes you feel very valued." Janet tells of dinners hosted by school supervisors or district leaders, where they invited various teachers and administrative staff, and "we all got to know each other in a different setting. So when big meetings came up and we needed to bring up something about curriculum or teaching methods or anything, they were more likely to really listen to my idea, and I was to theirs."

Yet there is still a division in how companies often think about and treat their employees based on perceived skill level. "We increasingly group the people in our firms into two classes:

those who have knowledge and talent and, by implication, those who do not," write John Hagel III, John Seely Brown, and Lang Davison, in the article, "Are All Employees Knowledge Workers?" in the *Harvard Business Review*. "This segmentation is misleading and damaging to firms in the long run."[3]

I agree. I grant that the very theme of this book – creating better employee experience – is geared much more to knowledge workers than to others. But belief and gratitude cannot be doled out in lopsided measures, based on title, compensation level, or visibility of task. Hagel, Brown, and Davison continue: "When executives focus on knowledge workers, they lose sight of the fact that even highly routinized jobs require improvisation and the use of judgment in ambiguous situations, especially if the goal is to drive performance to new levels."[4]

They note: "Perhaps the single greatest lesson from Japanese auto manufacturers is that all employees are ultimately knowledge workers and that the role of the firm is to both encourage and support problem-solving by all employees."[5]

This idea should permeate a company's entire leadership team. I would hope it does. In society today, so much focus is placed on our differences: our diverse backgrounds, socioeconomic status, and political affiliation. Finding as many areas for common ground as possible is crucial – and the dignity and necessity of our work efforts, all of our work efforts, is excellent ground to start.

Hagel, Brown, and Davison go on to explore the need to redefine how we perceive the most routine jobs if institutions and even nations are going to tap into the entire workforce. This enables performance achievement for everyone, not just knowledge workers.[6]

One way leaders can do that is to make sure that their entire workforce has equal access to learning, from entry-level on up, no matter where in the world they do their job. Creating opportunities and, as discussed, giving employees the agency and autonomy to pursue them, foster an environment where every person can bring their unique value to work. As leaders, it's our responsibility to help employees recognize their unique value. It may be an expertise or technical skill, but there is also tremendous value in "soft" skills like leadership, communication, problem-solving, and team-building. As I wrote earlier, there are people within every organization, maybe dozens, maybe hundreds, whose capabilities in these areas remain untapped.

Syad, now a division head for an engineering firm in Southeast Asia, was a long-time tech manager who had volunteered for a management program and then was named – before age 30, and somewhat to his shock – to a leadership HR position. Right away he felt he was in way over his head. "I had taken a one-day workshop in Singapore and in the taxi back to the hotel with the head of HR, I said, 'You've basically destroyed my career.' I had spent the day in a room full of HR leadership and they were all looking at me, this young lad, and I could see they were thinking, *We don't understand what he's trying to say, he doesn't understand what we're trying to say*. 'How is this going to work?' I asked my companion in the taxi. 'Give it time, you'll be all right,' he replied."

Syad was terrified – but he remembered the advice one of his peers had given him. "Don't play to their strengths, play to yours. Think of what you bring rather than trying to fit in."

Syad found those words to be life-changing. "I'm a techie, so I know numbers. I know how a business is run. The people I was afraid of were different, so I prepared a presentation titled, 'Run HR Like a Business.' I told them we could define measurable outcomes. That I would code real-time dashboards for them. That we could monitor and steer the HR organization in real time. None of what I said was anything they had ever heard, either there or across the company globally. In using my strength, I found my value. From then on, I just went from strength to strength. Six months after being totally terrified, I realized I had made myself indispensable to this new team."

Sometimes helping someone be the best version of themselves means recognizing their value – their gifts and their potential – and helping them to find the right role. The ability to recognize these strengths in employees, and encourage them to take risks, is critical as jobs become less rigid and more fluid and teams become more dynamic. If leaders can energize their employees to see their own value and pursue new opportunities, it will help them reach their fullest potential.

In many cases, an employee may not see the value they contribute. Women and other consistently underrepresented groups often have a more difficult job of valuing their own contributions. Rachel says, "It took a while to realize I have value. I've spent years working at my writing, understanding tone and how a style guide works, how narrative translates across different media. It feels like something that most people could do, so it didn't feel valuable to me." Working alongside talented people was inspiring to Rachel but also made her question further if what she did was really all that great. She helped to develop the brand voice for the company. "And because it was such a small team, I had a huge hand in everything, from the tone to the messaging to the pivot to a new market space, yet because I've always been a writer I didn't see what I was doing as a valuable skill. Not a big deal. For a long time, I didn't consider whether I was getting the best work experience or being compensated fairly. I wrote a pitch that we presented to a big venture capital firm, and at the end their head of marketing said, 'I don't get excited by million-dollar companies or one-hundred-million-dollar companies, I only get excited by billion-dollar companies – and you guys have a billion-dollar brand.' It was the brand she was interested in, not the product. I had done that. It was a startup and I should have gotten equity. I didn't ask because

I thought the proper etiquette was for them to offer it. Probably naïve of me. I don't know if the founders ever had a good understanding of the skill that I brought, or if they did and just didn't do right."

Companies need to recognize the value of their employees and communicate that. Sometimes it's in the form of pay or compensation, but there are other, still meaningful ways to acknowledge the value that people are bringing. As often as leaders are thinking of the company's value, that's how often they should think about the value of their employees. Ultimately, that value is what drives long-term growth and innovation.

Recognition Builds Culture

If you believe in people, and regularly and authentically express it, they have reason to stay with you and work hard for you. In *Leading at a Distance*, James M. Citrin and Darleen Derosa write that it is "vital to acknowledge employees' achievements . . . Even if they're separated by hundreds or thousands of miles, high-functioning virtual teams are still committed to both individual and collective success . . . Taking time to celebrate both individual performance and other wins can remind team members that each person's contributions matter to the team's success."[7]

It won't surprise you that, according to one study, "high-recognition companies" – which "build a culture of recognition through social reward systems (tools that give people points or kudos to reward to others), weekly or monthly thank-you activities, and a general culture of appreciating everyone from top to bottom" – have significantly "lower voluntary turnover than companies with poor recognition cultures."[8]

My one disagreement with the study – which also states that the "key to success here is to create a social environment where recognition can flow from peer to peer, freeing managers from being the judge and jury of employee recognition" – is the notion that managers can't or shouldn't be a vital part of recognition.[9] Having each and every employee feel valued can only make the business run better, and that recognition should come from every direction.

Recognition is about what you do. Appreciation is about who you are. The words are sometimes used interchangeably, but they always feel good.

Dani, a graphic designer at a mid-sized advertising firm, says, "There's a quality to the leadership team here that makes you want to do an even better job. I can't really put my finger on it. Honestly, I think it might just be respect."

Dahlia, a young doctor who moved from what she described as a "toxic" group practice environment to one that she loves, says, "I feel appreciated for what I do for them. They always say thanks for fitting this in, thanks for doing that. The doctors and technicians I work with are very appreciative of me being there and helping, and I never really felt that at my previous job. And I'm happy to help them. I'll work on my day off for someone else if they need to take a day. It rarely happens, but we all do that because we're all so grateful for each other and the general environment."

When leaders recognize behaviors, they reinforce culture. Those behaviors become embedded within the ethos of the company. Eventually, they become expected outputs.

Of course, this is also true when the behaviors being reinforced are flawed. "The culture I worked in previously was very much, for anyone below director level, 'Do the work, do the task in front of you, don't get too creative, don't try to solve problems even if you see them existing,'" says Molly, a former videographer for a giant media company who left to become a real estate agent. "There weren't structures for having conversations, so there weren't even structures for earning respect! We had none of those brainstorming sessions that my friends in tech tell me about, where the company leaders are soliciting ideas from everyone."

Doug, a salesperson for a tech company who has worked for several firms, has experienced the cutthroat, competitive approach and doesn't think it works better. "I don't believe you necessarily need to be comparing me with the guy sitting next to me all the time," he says. "Animosity builds. It makes me root against my peers. I already compare myself to my peers, so I don't need the company to throw it in my face and show everyone when I'm struggling to meet numbers or when my peers are struggling. We go through where we are for the quarter to know if we're on track for the year. You can see the numbers. I don't need you to stack-rank who's last or who needs to work harder, because there's a lot more than hard work that goes into what we do to succeed at sales. Timing is important. You could get a territory where the accounts already bought a ton of stuff last year. There's the territory itself. There's luck involved, frankly. Connecting with your customers at the right time and building those relationships. A little compassion and appreciation and understanding don't hurt."

Reinforcing the wrong behaviors diminishes recognition and appreciation. It impacts culture and what people are willing to produce or capable of producing. According to a survey from Great Place to Work, employees who feel recognized at work are two times more likely to say innovative thinking is embraced and people at their company are willing to go above and beyond.[10]

Sincere words are great. Actions that show how you feel are even greater. Martin, a tech executive, notes how, at one of his previous employers, "the CEO took people who may not have ever thought they would be president of a company, or even a division, and elevated them, which did two things: It built incredible loyalty, and it also told everyone else that they would be considered for promotion with an open mind."

Martin consulted for another company that "grew by acquisition, and their model was to get rid of all the top management and usually take the person who was running engineering and make them president of the division, which was then managed autonomously." That, too, sent a signal to employees who had rarely, if ever, considered themselves leadership material. Maybe they really were?

Is that new leader 100 percent ready for the job? Almost certainly not. Because no one is! As an HR leader once said to me, "As long as you're 50 percent ready, you'll learn on the job."

"The number-one thing is someone else's belief in you," she says. "They sponsored you, they gave you an opportunity. That's what matters most."

Lina, in the medical field, notes a small but significant "cultural kindness" in her company's way of doing things that made her, one of the more junior members of her company, feel important. "When we send letters to people for finishing their course and getting their certification, my signature is on the letter along with everybody else's from the company. And I'm tagged in every LinkedIn post on their website." It's not over-praising or inauthentic. "I play a role in how we're evolving and what direction we're going in and especially what gaps we're filling for patients." It makes her feel her value. It doesn't hurt that her senior colleagues also care about her life outside the office. "They compensate me well. They ask about my home because we just bought a new house. They ask about my husband and our dogs. I'm getting my master's and they always ask how school is going. These sound like such basic things, but they really are important, especially if you've gone into this field because you care about patients and people. And sadly, what I'm experiencing doesn't happen that often in the health care industry."

Celebrate the contribution – more importantly, celebrate the contributor, and connect the dots for others to show how the contributor's efforts made the whole company better, and maybe the world outside the company, too.

The Big Power of a Little Appreciation

To appreciate someone often requires so little.

When Anaya was starting at a law firm in India, she was understandably nervous, thinking on her first day, *Okay, what have I got myself into?* "That's when either you walk out or someone helps you navigate the system," she says. "And just to know that there's somebody who sees you – a simple 'Hello' or a 'How was your day yesterday?' makes a huge difference. I was lucky enough to have such a person. She was always there for me, amazingly. When I emailed her, she always replied quickly. That was my employee experience. It's just having someone there say, 'Yes, you matter.'"

Appreciation is not just a reward. It's also saying: I value you. I see you. I am glad to have you in my community. You belong here. We like having you here.

Nate, who works freelance in the film and advertising industry, has an easy rule of thumb for his encounters. It's the Golden Rule: Treat others as you would have them treat you. "I hire people and I get hired, so I'm conscious of making people feel valued – not just to be nice on my part but because I know how motivating it is, because it works on me. Each personality is different but I haven't met anyone yet who doesn't appreciate appreciation."

Appreciation builds loyalty. It builds trust. It builds respect. And it adds tremendous value to the business. While appreciation can take little effort, it has to be authentic. It doesn't hurt when it comes unexpectedly.

"Sometimes there will be a note of praise on a Google doc that the whole team will see, and those are nice," says Rachel, the writer. "But when I started working here and I'd done my first couple rounds of projects, I heard from the producer I was working under that the head of strategy, one of the partners, said during their weekly all-hands-on-deck meeting that he wanted everyone to know that they had found a new writer, her name is Rachel, she's incredible, and if any of you need support on a project, reach out to her. And I wasn't in the meeting! It wasn't done for show. That to me was really special."

One team leader I know devotes the start of every weekly team meeting to "Snaps and Claps."

"I ask, 'Who has a personal win they want to share?'" she says. "We snap and clap for interns who are finishing their dissertation. We might snap and clap to thank someone for helping a colleague with a task. Or any milestone. It's a habit we've developed, and this way you don't have to wait too long to celebrate things. We have personal wins, we have team wins." She tells me that it was just "Snaps" for a long time, until "one of our team members said they didn't know how to snap their fingers, so we said we would create a reasonable accommodation." Enter "Claps."

We all want to look good. When we make people look good by praising them honestly for their efforts, we feel good. They feel more connected to us and to the common goal. It's a virtuous circle. None of this is to suggest that appreciation be over-the-top or disconnected to real achievement – or insincere. If it were any of those, it wouldn't succeed at its task. Managers have different styles and personalities, and it's possible to genuinely appreciate someone without being a Ted Lasso type. Indeed, one of the great characters on the TV show is the end-of-his-career soccer superstar Roy Kent, who is as prickly as Ted Lasso is cuddly. When Roy is moved to appreciate someone, in his gruff, profane way, it may count for even more.

"I don't need the new cheerleading, everything-is-sunshine-and-rainbows management style," says Richard, a project manager. "I personally work best under individuals who do not tell me that everything I produce is perfect. And I think there's a misconception among today's management and leaders, many of whom think that the younger generations are incapable of receiving feedback that's direct, constructive, and/or critical. By far the best leader I ever worked for told me, the first time I delivered work to her, 'What you did kind of isn't all that great' – then immediately showed me ways to improve. It was that feedback loop I yearned for, because if you don't get it, then where are you? In the dark. If all you're hearing is 'Great job!' then that's problematic. By taking the time to show me how I could do better, she was basically telling me I was worth her time and effort."

I am not advocating for the often-mocked "participation medal" when the job performed isn't actually good. Genuine praise – delivered in whatever style comes most naturally, but also in a way that will resonate with the person who merited it – helps everyone. It's a virtuous circle.

Certainly, there are employees in many roles in many companies in many industries who are made to feel that *they* are the ones who should be appreciative. "There's a sense in this industry that you should be grateful for what you have because there would be a line out the door for your job," says Katherine, who works in film production. "The anyone-would-be-lucky-to-be-in-your-shoes narrative is felt pretty widely by everyone entering the industry. And yeah, I feel legitimately lucky to have this job. I'm getting paid and there's someone who seeks my creative input. But there's also very little chance of being promoted for a long time, and it's hard to feel stable at this level, especially if you're in independent production. There's no guarantee even at the studios. I've been talking to the same assistant at one studio for the past four years and he's older than me and hasn't changed his position."

The idea that appreciation and recognition should seem like a perk rather than a given is counterproductive to any positive business goal a company puts forth. In so many of the interviews conducted for this book, people smiled over their positive employee experience only because the present was so different from their recent employment past. "I would say right now I'm the happiest in my career," says Hillary. "I love working for this startup. Our CEO has a really wonderful leadership personality that you don't come across very often. He's always appreciative and thankful. Every time he thanks me for doing things, I have to admit, I still find it kind of shocking."

A company that neglects the human element has a completely different culture, thus a completely different company. When that element is added – transforming the company culture into one of appreciation, recognition, gratitude, and belief – it breeds a far better experience for the workforce, and significantly increases the odds of attracting great talent, keeping them happy, and building a thriving organization.

People will rise to what you believe in them to do.

A culture of recognition is good for business, especially for attracting talent and keeping it.

One-on-one appreciation is nice. Public praise is more impactful.

III

Foundations for a Great Employee Experience

We desperately need more leaders who are committed to courageous, wholehearted leadership and who are self-aware enough to lead from their hearts rather than unevolved leaders who lead from hurt and fear.

Brené Brown

Authentic Beats Perfect

Leadership Today

I've always believed that you enjoy working for a company because you enjoy working for your boss. And that the whole culture of the company is reflected in your direct boss.

— Manager #1

The onus on managers to keep employees' interest alive is way more challenging now. You're a little square on a screen. I can't read your body language. You can't read mine. You might be bored out of your skull talking to me right now. You could be excited. You could be thinking, "When is this damn woman going to hang up?"

— Manager #2

We as a company, as leaders, as managers have to understand that people aren't motivated by the things they were in the past. It's not enough to dangle that promotion or raise or end-of-year bonus – I mean, those things are important, but I look at Alison, a superstar, and what a shame it would be if we did anything that made her go work elsewhere. The most important thing in her life is her three-year-old son. We have to accommodate that to retain her as a productive employee. We have to think in new ways about not only is experience important, but what kinds of experience? It depends on the industry but ours isn't one where you punch a clock, put in your time, count the number of widgets at the end of the day. We're in an industry where having people with diverse backgrounds, who are endlessly curious – they're gems. If we don't provide the kind of experience to retain those gems, we'll lose them.

— Manager #3

Think of the best leader you know. Or the best manager. (In this chapter, I'll use "manager" and "leader" somewhat interchangeably, though I wouldn't use "manager" to mean the head of the whole organization.) Think of the best boss you know.

Have them in mind? Good. Maybe the memory makes you smile. Maybe – even better! – it's not a memory and you're thinking of your current boss.

Now, when you think of that person, what traits come to mind?

Kindness? Enthusiasm? Good humor, energy, boldness, fairness? Most virtues are timeless, and you or anyone would have found them appealing in a boss whether they were your direct superior at a software firm way back in 2017, or your supervisor while you were grinding grain at a mill in 3rd-century Rome. People are people.

But because of the many forces that are transforming the employee experience that I discussed in Chapter 1, especially for those we call knowledge workers, and because of epic changes in the larger culture, the leader profile has shifted, too.

"The image of the 'ideal leader' has changed quite a lot," says Frances Botha, SAP-APJ's Human Resources head. "It used to be it was the one who could speak perfectly, who had this perfect message about mission and vision and strategy, and they would talk and everyone listening would be going *Yes, yes, yes*. These days, employees like managers who are more vulnerable. It's fine when a manager says, 'You know what? I totally messed up.' Or 'I myself struggle with this.' Not just fine – *admired*. When leaders talk like that, people will say, 'She's so real, he's so real. I can identify with them.' Nowadays, they're looking for that in their leaders. Not someone who's so perfect you can't relate."

I couldn't agree more.

The ascendancy of vulnerability as a positive trait, one that we admire not just in our fellow human being but in people who might lead us, is not some fly-by-night, touchy-feely observation. It's actually rooted in data. Brené Brown – podcaster, author, deeply curious and humanistic academic – conducted years of research about human connection. She found, among other things, that "the main concern about connection emerged as the fear of disconnection; the fear that something we've done or failed to do, something about who we are or where we come from, has made us unlovable and unworthy of connection. . . . we resolve this concern by understanding our vulnerabilities and cultivating empathy, courage, and compassion."[1]

"Telling it like it is" is an appropriate motto for this Age of Transparency and Vulnerability.

I'm burned out. I've struggled for months to find boundaries between work and home life. It's impacting my focus, productivity, and general well-being. There are too many meetings and not enough time to think and create. Increasing needs and changing expectations (both at work and at home) have become exhausting. No one can do it all, but we all want to try.

You know who wrote that? Me. It was the opening paragraph of a blog I posted on October 10, 2021, World Mental Health Day, as good an occasion as any for me, as the leader of a large team, to confess publicly my own issues, fears, and failings.

The post received more comments than any I had ever written. The conversation it started was healthy, too. People opened up and shared their own tips for fighting burnout and staying healthy and productive.

Showing vulnerability is not a mark against anyone, including leaders. It now can be liberating, not suffocating. Nor does it keep one from acting boldly. "Research shows that when managers have a track record of challenging the status quo, they tend to be more open to new ideas and less threatened by contributions from others," says Adam Grant. "They care more about making the organization better than about defending it as it stands."[2]

In the past, vulnerability in a leader registered as a weakness; there was a cost to sharing something candid and not immediately favorable. Employees wouldn't see them as strong as they did before.

That's not true today.

Vulnerability is not the only trait trending up. Along with and connected to it is authenticity. Where once certain traits were prized as classic "leadership" qualities (command and control, knowing it all, motivation through fear), today authenticity is essential if a leader is to be taken seriously. It's an outgrowth – a very positive one, in my opinion – of the far more transparent, accountable, connected world we live in. If you're thinking of trying to get away with something, or that you can act in a way that's not really you, think again. There are channels to call that out that didn't exist before.

Authenticity is a prerequisite, as compulsory as the references you provide on a résumé.

Peter, in sales, left a startup months ago because it was done in by a lack of authenticity. "A lot of the problems hidden in the background were rooted in the management style. 'Real' means that every part of it has to work together to achieve its purpose. If you're only trying to build this façade, this show, then eventually it will all topple and collapse."

Anand was plucked from his engineering job to be a manager leading the team he had just been part of; unfortunately he didn't handle the transition well. "I had been recognized for my performance, and since it was my team, I knew the business inside and out. That was my strength but also my peril because as a manager, when someone would come to me with a problem, I could tell right away whether it was a content issue or an excuse or BS. I knew I couldn't be too rough on people so I started acting plasticky. I had no idea how to be or who I was. I ended up basically fixing things myself, doing the work of ten people, a lot of micromanagement, nothing that could ever possibly scale."

What is the lesson from Anand's story? Managers need guiding principles for leadership that include reminding them of the basics but also the value of authenticity. Anand needed to encourage his team to share stories and lessons learned so that they could grow and improve (and he wouldn't always be left with the extra "fix-it" work).

Another of my personal favorites from the "Which Leadership Traits Might Be More Important in Today's World?" album: kindness.

"As leaders we need to remember that we're all human," says a division head based in India. "We all have our own problems, and sometimes, unfortunately, we carry them to the workplace. So everyone should get the benefit of the doubt. A person comes in all crabby and you want to think, *Oh, what a horrible person that is*. But you don't know what they're going through or what just happened. They could have had a fight with their partner. Their kid might have had an emotional morning. Their parents are ill. Maybe it's just that they stubbed their toe ten seconds before walking in. Not a big deal, but it still hurts, right?"

We work on our skills, our education, our place in the pecking order. Do we actively work on becoming more empathetic?

A good employee experience includes the feeling that others are sensitive to the experiences that the employee is having, good or bad. The employee wants to know that their manager appreciates their situation. This starts by managers being open about their own experiences. It's not okay to whine, but we definitely bond through sharing the trials and tribulations we face in the often difficult world we all share.

"I know it sounds crazy," continues the division leader, "but I honestly believe that extra empathy can make or break a company."

Managers Have It Tough

Managers play a critical role in employee experience because they are the face of the company to most of its employees. A company cannot actually care for a person. Only a person can care for another person, which is why the behavior of the manager and other leaders is critical to employee experience.

Managers have a lot to contend with. There are individual differences in the people that managers manage. There are generational differences to contend with. Managers are also "stuck" between two groups – the expectations of their own superior and those of their employees. Managers are required to align these considerations when they simply might not. Leaders want more productivity at less cost; meanwhile, employees want more resources and more realistic expectations for their workload. The manager is stuck in the middle.

And here's something else, specific to our era: The speed of life has never been faster. With the social, global, and technological upheavals of the past few years, and with the labor and educational markets widely imbalanced in some key areas, new issues have emerged.

"Managers should do less, manage more, lead more," says one HR leader. "Be more involved in the people element."

Like it or not, managers convey the culture of the company, by themselves and also through the people they influence. Managers must make decisions and support behaviors that reinforce an organization's values on issues like safety, diversity, equity and inclusion, well-being, and environmental sustainability. Since organizational culture impacts both business performance and candidate attraction, a lot rests on the manager.

And managers drive strategy. To do that, they need to deeply understand the strategy, to be a great communicator, and to know how to mentor. To mentor requires a longer-term investment, with a focus on each of their employees' career development.

Given all they're responsible for, and given all the vulnerability that managers are now allowed, they're going to make mistakes. They're human.

I believe there are three distinct duties that *every manager and leader must carry out* to establish an environment where employees can learn, grow, and thrive:

- **Drive Clarity of Purpose:** Know the mission and purpose of the company, empower individual employee strengths, and connect those to the purpose of the company, so everyone knows their why as part of the greater why.

- **Create Connection:** Model respect for one another, help one another, build up one another, and believe in each other to accomplish great things.

- **Require Transparency and Build Trust:** Create a culture of openness and honesty in feedback, with the intention of supporting growth and innovation.

These may sound like "motherhood and apple pie" elements that are more than obvious, but studies have shown the value of strongly engaging cultures for fostering innovation and growth.

Today's workers will not tolerate an organization without these elements. And those are just the start.

Managers tend to operate based on how they are managed by their own leaders. If leaders want better managers, then leaders need to become better managers themselves.

Style *Is* Substance

They say that movie directors and baseball umpires are at their best when we don't notice they're even there. That can be true for some of the best managers, too. Matt, a tech executive, told of this exchange with one of his first bosses, "a very approachable guy."

"Dave, you're the best boss I've ever had," said Matt.

"Really?" said Dave. "Why is that?"

"Well, because you let me make my mistakes and learn from them."

"What mistakes did you make?"

After thinking it over for a bit, Matt said, "Honestly, I don't think I've really made any big mistakes."

Dave nodded. "Matt, that's why I'm the best boss you ever had. Because you *think* I let you make mistakes."

The lesson Matt took from the exchange: He had benefited from a boss who trusted him, who was empathetic, and who spent the time to understand what worked best for him. Matt admitted that before Dave was his boss, he "wasn't great with authority." Dave used a different approach from most managers. Rather than meeting with him just once a month and telling him, "Okay, these are the 15 tasks you need to get done," Dave initiated conversations about the work to be done, trust-based conversations that gave Matt the opportunity to think things over and, where he had a difference of opinion, suggest new approaches to the work. Matt felt respected. He also felt "as if I was part of something because we were successful and I had contributed to that success in more than just my daily tasks."

Managers today must be master accommodators, enabling an environment and psychological ambience so that each and every one of their employees will work hard and feel good about it. One manager I know made the effort to tailor her meetings to each of her direct reports' individual preferences. "One of them likes nature so we've had meetings while walking in the park nearby, talking about the development plan. Another one loves a beer so we've met now and then at a bar. Another one loves to read so I got her a book before our last meeting. Another one loves a good croissant so we meet at a pastry shop. I really think of each person's taste and experiences, because if you want to build a relationship and it's always the same environment, and not at all on their terms . . . this just shows the extra effort. I don't think it's lost on them."

Not that today's employees are shy about speaking up for what they want. "My friend Megan was on a project she hated," says Chloe, in media, "and during her weekly stand-up with the head of strategy, she just blurted out, 'I don't know how much longer I can do this project because I hate it.' Her manager said, 'Okay.' He listened to her complaint. Later, she found out that, behind the scenes, her manager had moved things around, talked to a few people in a low-key way, and without fireworks took her off the project. There was no 'Hey, everyone! Megan doesn't want to be on this project anymore!' I shouldn't be surprised because her company really takes care of their people, very big on making sure you have good work-life balance. It's an intense, creative industry, and I know of competitors where it's considered cool and inspiring if you never take a break, never rest, never take time off, never sleep. Her company is really good at tending to human needs and the whole employee experience."

There's another lesson here that should not be missed: Taking care of an employee's needs without calling attention to it can be the best way to earn trust. Calling out the remedial action in a group setting can make the employee uncomfortable, but respecting a valid request and acting on it without fanfare builds trust.

Evie says, "There's one technician that I really don't get along with, and I get along with most people. I told my manager straight up, 'I don't want to work with her. It's not good for me as a new hire. My confidence level goes down when I work with her.' They made sure not to schedule me with her anymore." If a manager has the key to making an employee happier, or less unhappy, nothing should get in the way of doing it as soon as possible. The beneficiary won't forget.

To share concerns, the employee needs to feel psychologically safe with their manager, so that there's trust between them, and the manager can give honest feedback that the employee will take in the right spirit. "You need to feel safe with the person to have a real conversation with them, and it goes both ways," says one HR manager. "And I think that's where the magic starts. It takes investment. Some managers just haven't made the investment to develop that type of relationship with their employees."

With young employees or those early in their time with a company, things can occasionally overwhelm them. The empathetic manager finds a way. "Sometimes the employee doesn't need a mentor for that," says one manager. "They need a friend."

It has become standard in some circles to portray the younger generation of workers as entitled, coddled, self-absorbed. Mostly this is coming from clickbait media platforms. Some of the hardest workers in my company are fresh out of college or a little older. They don't hold back with sharing their expectations – but I also see a willingness to listen in a way that is inspiring and hugely healthy. Leaders in turn must listen and know when they're needed. "I try to let people make their own decisions, but at the same time I keep them away from sharp objects whenever I can," says one executive. "If it's a business issue, I'll try to direct them to their manager, so that I'm not micromanaging anyone on the team." There's a healthy and productive alternative to micromanaging: macromanaging. "When you macromanage," writes Janet Britcher, "you set clear expectations and define how performance will be measured. You welcome input and are willing to tweak the process. . . . the key . . . is nothing more than inquiry."[3]

Some employees prefer leaders *not* to be so subtle in their approach. "I really like when leadership is highly visible, and their excitement for what we're doing is clear and they know how to share their vision," says Janet, a teacher, acknowledging that her work culture is very different from a corporate one – but maybe not as different as one might think. "I like to know the vision, from principals and district supervisors. Sometimes I've had to ask, 'Could we have a little State of the Union?' Especially when someone new comes into leadership, you want to know what's important to them, what they value, and help get the entire staff excited about it. I work best when people share their views, when I know my role, and when I know we're on the same page."

There are different styles to driving purpose – behind the scenes, being out front – but whatever style a manager chooses, it should be clear.

Empowering and Unleashing Potential

I have always had a deep gratitude and great admiration for those who teach. Good teachers inspire you. They make you think differently and help you discover your strengths. They help you unleash your potential.

Leaders have the great opportunity to teach – to help others discover their amazing potential along their learning journey. For me, this is one of the greatest joys of work: watching others attain and exceed their own expectations of themselves.

Or, as Brinda, a division leader, puts it, "The essence of my leadership is, 'How do I make others successful?'"

At SAP, our leaders focus on career trajectory and skills development. Many of them have a standing call to talk with their employees about career aspirations and how we can help prepare them for the next role. We have programs that give high performers opportunities to work on challenging, impactful projects that give them direct access to our top leadership. We share the success stories from these projects to highlight their work and let others know what's possible. Participants in these programs have commented that the access to leadership was one of the most valuable aspects of the program. Particularly at a large company, access to leaders is crucial. The benefit is bidirectional: It's a direct communication channel for our leadership to shape company culture and it's a way for employees to share their work and inspire our leaders.

Everyone needs someone to believe in them. Seeing talent and promise in people under you, formulating a progression plan, reminding the person that they're going places (because they are, though they may not quite know it yet), giving them projects to grow and stretch, providing feedback, finding the best communication style that works for both leader and employee: These remain some of the most exciting parts of leading a team. People will make mistakes, but a leader can reframe the situation and focus on the learning and growth. As human beings we need hope and belief that the future is promising. A good manager can give someone new hope and vision for their future by asking a few simple questions and showing that leadership believes in its people, such as:

What do you want to do?

I see you're really great at x. Where can we take it?

Where do you want your career to go?

Have you considered a fellowship to try that out?

In a compassionate, encouraging company setting, these are the questions we leaders should be asking all the time of our employees. Recently I heard someone say that the "E" in CEO should stand for Experience. Maybe the E in CEO should stand for Encouragement: Chief Encouragement Officer.

"When I started my job, work was still fully virtual because of the pandemic," says Toni, "and I had weekly one-on-ones with my manager. We'd just try to get to know each other in small, insignificant ways, whether it was just talking about our dogs who walked across the screen, or our hair appointments, or whatever. I think leadership starts with an understanding of what new employees are going through, especially during times of change and uncertainty."

Managers teach. Managers empower. Managers shape behaviors and culture. Managers give their teams an ability to see positive outcomes and a brighter future.

The (Dreaded) Meeting and Other Gatherings

How do employees prefer to gather today? There's no one best way that has yet emerged in the third decade of the 21st century. Some are one-on-one fans. Some merely go through the motions of the somewhat artificially mandated weekly or monthly one-on-one, preferring a call or communication as needed. As one manager pointed out, "I don't love the idea that people wait until a one-on-one to tell you something you probably should have known a week ago." Though more meetings happen virtually, of course, nothing about the variety of gatherings is particularly special to today's era.

What *can* be increasingly challenging – and it's something I experienced in my time in Asia – is fitting the objective of the meeting to the type of gathering with the right environment and tone. A colleague whose work travels have taken him to many destinations says, "I have people in India, China, Australia, Hungary, Ireland, Scotland, and of course the States. Culturally, there are lots of differences to manage. In India, when I had my first one-on-one meetings with team members, several of them insisted on preparing a slide deck. I told them no, no, it was just a get-to-know-you, we can talk about our families and hobbies and backgrounds, very informal. 'There's nothing to prepare,' I assured them. 'You don't need to bring slides.' Of course, several people brought slides. They felt more comfortable. It was actually quite touching." Leaders looking to make great and comfortable employee experiences for global teams will increasingly need to account for these nuances.

Larger gatherings are key for clearly articulating your company's purpose, strategy, and goals. Done well, they can help employees connect their own role to the company's purpose and foster a sense of camaraderie. These gatherings can present challenges, too. One finance manager shared a story about a quarterly business review with the president of his company and several other senior leaders. "He was so harsh toward the Head of Sales. She hadn't made her numbers, through no fault of hers, but he just berated her, he implied she was the worst employee in the entire company, that she was such a failure, not putting forth effort, and just went on and on. It was hard to watch. It was not only a horrible experience for her but for the rest of the team, too. He lost the respect of so many of us in that one meeting."

Leaders can impact the entire organization with condescending or disrespectful behavior toward just one person when there is a large audience. Large meetings have their place, but the messages they convey should be thoughtful and intentional. As a general rule, discipline and correction should be done in private. You cannot create a growth-mindset culture when people are afraid of being embarrassed in front of their peers. Such a culture can be achieved only when the employee feels safe enough to share their own failure and lesson.

One consultant I know with a background in psychology worked with a large utility company, spending a great deal of time helping them on error management and continuous improvement, which she says "is really rooted in psychological safety. You need to be able to communicate when you've made a mistake. And when you work in utilities, it's *really* important to communicate when near-misses have happened." She implemented a program:

a weekly call for the entire division, made up of hundreds of managers, with the intention of sharing mistakes, near-misses, and addressing them. "I watched some of the managers prepare, as it came their turn to speak, because something had happened in their unit," says the consultant. "They literally looked nauseous – anxious, sweating, shaking. That wasn't the intention. The point of the meeting was to surface errors and learn from them. But it was turning into more of a firing squad of those who had to share information in this setting. They didn't feel basic psychological safety, even among their team, much less the executives they were getting in front of and sharing their mistakes."

When she thought about how to improve the situation, her dealings with a smaller company she knew gave her an idea. "It was a very loose, casual group, unabashed by language, and once someone in that group made an error and had no trouble saying, 'I f***** up.' Soon enough, it became a thing, and we started every meeting, including with managers, with a round of 'Who F***** Up?' We realized it made bonding and communication so much more real and immediate. We didn't just use 'Who F***** Up?' for major things, but even little things. We didn't do it as leaders and direct reports but as peers and colleagues. Just raise your hand and say, 'I f***** up! This did not go well, we made this mistake, and this is the outcome of it.' We could all learn from the mistake and it made it easier for others to share."

Creating a weekly or somewhat regular habit like this requires trust among a team and cultivates more trust. Managers can build from that groundswell of energy and comfort. It's easier to do this around people you work with every day; it may be less easy to involve senior leadership in the effort. But building a culture of trust requires a level of vulnerability from all.

How does a manager balance everyone's needs in a virtual group meeting? How does one ensure that everyone feels comfortable speaking up? A manager wants to help the whole team feel safe and valued. When I meet with large groups of employees based all over the world, including in time zones half a day away, I try to schedule two sessions, one morning and one night, so people know we respect their time as much as possible.

My checklist for leaders looking to plan an impactful meeting that provides a positive experience:

1. Clearly state the purpose of the meeting prior to the start.
2. Be intentional about whom you invite, and acknowledge the audience and its purpose.
3. Have an agenda that helps you achieve the intended purpose and outcome.
4. Be human: Show empathy and consider how the message affects the people gathered.
5. Before the meeting, ask yourself this: How do you want your audience to feel when they leave the meeting?

This last point helps you set the tone. And as I wrote above, style sometimes *is* substance. Tone can mean the difference between a successful meeting and one where people walk away irritated, resentful, and distracted.

Transparency and Trust

In leadership, there's nothing more important than transparency and trust.

With trust and transparency established, a company is well on the way to a great culture, one that works particularly well for today's workforce. If things change, as they inevitably will in any organization, then a leader who communicates clearly and truthfully, fully and without undue delay, will still preserve the goodwill of the people – maybe more so, since they can transparently appreciate the full set of what is being navigated.

Francis, a worker in occupational safety, felt respected because his manager wanted him to better understand the business. "He wants me to learn more about the financial side. He feels it's important, and I agree. To succeed in my role, which is to reduce workplace injuries, I need to learn more about the projects themselves and what is at risk. If I also have an understanding about the costs, I'll be better able to do my job. Today, I go into every day thinking, 'Let's not get hurt. I don't care how much it costs.'" If the financials of the company are more transparent to Francis, then he will be more conscious of his part in the broader business and deliver better results.

Trust and transparency are two crucial inputs to a great company culture. The Great Place to Work Institute lists six elements of a superior company culture:

1. Community
2. Fairness
3. Trustworthy Management
4. Innovation
5. Trust
6. Caring[4]

That's a lot. But if the leadership approach stems from a basic humanity, compassion, and respect for one another, no matter where on the org chart (if there even is one), then such a culture is within reach, and strong, supportive relationships will flourish throughout the company.

People Don't Quit Companies

Glitches happen even in good company cultures. At the top of the list, perhaps, is this one: the bad manager.

Or this one: A leader gets antsy and moves on to another division or project, leaving the team to build trust and rhythm with a new leader.

Things go wrong in the best cultures. It's true wherever there are humans and organizations. Sometimes, certain people are just not right for other people.

More frequently than I'd like, I hear a "manager from hell" story. Karen had such a manager. Karen felt unsure about what was expected of her. She was given no clear objectives. When she turned in work, she got no feedback. When she asked for feedback, she was told it was coming and it never did. Then she'd be given another assignment, always a rush, and once she turned it in, it too was ignored. Karen's manager had made no attempt to get to know her better. A better employee experience for Karen wasn't at the top of her manager's list.

All was not hopeless, though. Karen knew that the company's assessment mechanism would kick in. When it came time for Karen and other employees (also at their wit's end) to rate the manager's performance, the system would do what it was designed to, and leadership would understand what Karen and others had been enduring.

On the assessment survey scale, the best a manager could score was 100. Karen's manager scored a –25. That's not a typo. That's *negative 25*. It almost defied logic.

Yet Karen's manager stayed right where she was. How? For reasons only partly shared with Karen, her manager was "protected" because she was performing well in another area of the business and seen as a top revenue producer, though her "leadership" and people skills were terrible.

Why recount this at all? Karen eventually found her way to another position in the company, with a manager she loves and who loves her back. But there's this: "I have PTSD [posttraumatic stress disorder] from working with my last manager," says Karen. "I get very anxious about sending off work, even when, deep down, I know it's high quality. When I have one-on-ones with my current manager, who's lovely, I'll say to him, 'How am I doing? Am I doing okay? Am I dropping the ball? Did you like my proposal? Was the design okay?' And he'll say, 'You need to relax. Everything's great. You're doing a great job.'"

One responsibility of top leadership is to make sure that bad managers don't happen. But of course they do. We're human. Systems are flawed. So when a bad manager *does* happen, they need to be reassigned as soon as possible. Because the effect that the relationship has on employees can last a lot longer than the unfortunate time they spend together.

There is a common belief that employees don't quit companies, they quit managers. There is more to this story. Employees quit companies that employ and tolerate lousy managers.

As one senior executive at a multinational firm says soberly, "You have to lead through empathy and trust, for sure. Everybody says that. Unfortunately, not everybody does that."

TAKE THIS WITH YOU

Managers, the culture carriers of a company, are more important than the C-suite.

Authentic beats perfect.

When you leave a meeting, know how you made them feel.

CHAPTER

Collaboration at Work

Humane Technology

There's a popular French bakery in a college town that employs lots of college kids – cashiers, stock clerks, assistant store managers. The lowest position is slicer-bagger.

"It's a boring job," says Robert, the bakery's co-owner. "But it's an opportunity to get in, see what you might like to do. If you want to learn how to bake, you have the chance to work with our lead baker, a French fellow who's been doing it for 35 years and loves to teach people. Slicer-bagger is a low-paying entry job, but if you enjoy doing it, it's easy to move up and become a baker and earn more money."

Not long ago, Robert faced a predicament: Should he buy a slicing-bagging machine? "It would take care of all that and pay for itself in a year," he says. "But then I thought: Is that really what we want to do? Or do we want to have an entry-level job opportunity for new people to grow and learn? It's a great way to get people in the door. If I buy the slicing/bagging machine, then I close the door a bit on finding good people."

Robert is a rare businessperson.

Nearly every company, it seems, is branding or rebranding itself as a technology company, regardless of the industry sector it appears to belong to – retail, packaged goods, cars, laundry detergent, jelly donuts. In a world in which anything high tech is seen as faster, smarter, more efficient – *better* – it makes sense to position yourself as one of them; it may do wonders for your stock price, at least initially. (In 2017, the beverage maker Long Island Iced Tea Corp., in the midst of a particularly intense run-up in the price of Bitcoin and other cryptocurrencies, announced it was changing its name to Long Blockchain Corp. Its share price immediately jumped 200 percent.)[1]

Though many businesses believe that to survive and thrive they must be "tech-first" companies, I would suggest that every viable company in the future will be a "people-first" company.

To improve employee experience, leaders will want to highlight the human element. As I've written, qualities like meaning, recognition, connecting, relating, teaching, learning, and nurturing the whole self are the ones most deeply sought and embraced by today's employees. That's not to say that technology doesn't have a prime place in delivering that value, because it does. We well know, for example, that connecting, teaching, and learning are all powerfully aided by technological developments. But as we enter the next tech phase, one in which artificial intelligence, robotics, and job automation become even more pervasive and potentially threatening to a large segment of workers and businesses, it's helpful to look at business leaders out there like Robert, the ones who don't *automatically* opt for the machine solution, because it's not always the best answer – from a human *or* business perspective.

The People Part

SAP's onboarding program comes with a person. That's right. All new hires are assigned a buddy, your go-to person. You can ask them anything. "I remember asking my buddy, 'How do I get my laptop?' and 'Where's the pantry?'" says Suki, now a leader in one of our Asia offices. "'Where do I sit?' It was that basic. The first week was just handholding. The whole buddy experience was really important." It's a human touch, but there's technology to support it.

As more and more employees used the system, we made it more interactive and casual. We made it region-specific; before, you might be in Singapore and go through the virtual onboarding segment of the process with a person in San

Francisco, which made little sense. (It did at the time.) Now, new employees in Singapore get virtually onboarded in Singapore, with their new peers. As new salespeople begin selling, our technology provides them with the value proposition of the offering, the nuances, any changes coming, anything that could help our customers make a more informed decision. Suki says, "It helps me explain to the customer why they should buy this, and the reason it's going to improve their life."

Technology should be helpful. Can it also be humane? Yes, absolutely. If we examine just how it positively affects employee experience, then yes. It's easy to paint a picture of automation as cold and heartless, but I don't believe that. Why? I think that the greater efficiencies that new technology offers are about as "people first" as it gets.

I learned to code and create technical designs. But early in my career I realized that whatever gifts I had didn't include building the technology; my strength was in communicating what the technology could do for our clients. I could share and explain the future tech vision with the CFO of a giant Texas utility in a way that none of my colleagues could because they weren't using the right words. I could break things down to the core elements of what was relevant to the client and then put it into their words, their terminology, their context. I did that for a long time. I loved it.

I believe that we mischaracterize innovation when we make it seem as if it's separate from, or even in opposition to, human beings and humanity. After all, what *is* "innovation"? It's another way of saying "human ingenuity." When someone says they have faith in innovation, they really mean they have faith in human ingenuity, in human creativity. When our SAP SuccessFactors partners say, "We want to co-innovate with you," they mean they're looking for a technological solution to an existing problem. What they *really* mean, I believe, is that they want us both to find ways for smart human beings in our respective companies to come up with an amazing idea, then use technology to implement it, so that we can answer a human need. That's innovation, pure and simple. It's not a gadget we find under a rock, which then miraculously makes work more efficient so that we can have a 30-hour workweek instead of a 40-hour one. It's addressing the need for more and more people to work flexibly, often from home. It's figuring out a better scheduling algorithm so that a single parent-gig worker without a car can choose the best shifts for their schedule, in the least disruptive way possible. Innovation is smart people coming up with the idea for Zoom and implementing it, to meet the needs of millions.

COVID-19 and the accelerated move toward remote and hybrid work did not make us less human because we all swapped out in-person encounters for small-face-to-small-face screen meetings on Zoom and Teams and other virtual meeting places. (When we ditched commuting, didn't we just swap one set of technologies – planes, trains, and automobiles – for increased use of another – laptops and phones?) In virtual work, we discovered that people are still the most important part of the equation. Technology connects us because we're humans and we need to connect. We need people to work with. Part of our SAP SuccessFactors design team is responsible for innovating and building our software. This team works in productive groups, even as they're scattered across India, Germany, California, and elsewhere. They come together to figure out how their ideas can fit together. One executive just returned from "an incredible virtual event with ten thousand attendees from the U.S. and the Americas and nine thousand more from Europe, the Middle East, and Africa. Well-produced, some prerecorded content like product roadmaps, with live sessions, live interviews, live questions from the audience, then breakout sessions so you could go to different rooms." The collaborative spirit is not just on the end user side of the screen but also in those who create the experiences: We ship code to our customers for their learning initiatives, but it's the code that they, the clients, build around that initial code that makes it work best for them.

In his book, *The Gap*, Thomas Suddendorf states that what makes us different from the animal world is our capacity to coordinate our actions, understand a vision, and, through our language, collaborate to achieve a shared long-term goal.[2] In short: What makes us human is what makes us successful. AI works "merely" when it understands how our brains work and how we think and what we do, and ultimately helps us to do it a little faster, and also do more of the boring, repetitive stuff. It doesn't replace the human element. It enables it.

Give and Take

Other developments or predicted trends, though, seem more ambiguous in their "people-first" value. Will "superjobs" – defined as "positions combining tasks once performed by people in two or more traditional roles," perhaps comprising as many as 20 to 30 percent of future jobs – lead to a large swath of workers suddenly out of work and ill-equipped for new employment?[3] The good news is that there will still be a need for humans in the job. Automation will take over rote tasks, but those parts of the job that can be done only by humans will merge with other jobs, and one person will do this superjob. For the lucky, skilled ones who land such work, superjobs will likely pay more.

And it's hard to know what to make of this: Research has found that "less than 5 percent of occupations can be automated in their entirety."[4]

Much as we wish to automate anything and everything, did the advent of fitness monitoring device Fitbit really make people walk more? Or just have a talking point about how much they walked? As much as virtual gatherings have taken some of the edge off of the heightened isolation and disconnectedness of the last couple of years . . . we still crave the live, in-person presence of others with whom to eat meals, have happy hour, toss a football, take a walk, do yoga. Good thing we have dogs, right?

The experiences are just not the same. Too much screen time can make one's employee experience feel as if it's all an extension of work, rather than a blending of work and non-work.

The use of technology is a give and take. It has helped our mental health, and it has harmed it. Let's take social media, for example: A platform built for sharing and connectedness leads to a feeling of isolation for those who use it most. The platforms are designed to be addictive and are associated with anxiety, depression, and even physical ailments, according to a report from Harvard Medical School.[5]

Tech can make the world smaller, and it can make it impossibly large and complex. It can teach children all sorts of things they want to know, right away, and it has undeniably shortened their attention spans.

It has relieved us of many annoying repetitive tasks . . . which we have replaced by tapping our finger on a button repeatedly to win a game or answer a question or see the next news story we're not interested in or refreshing our email that we checked just a minute before.

How do we leverage technology, both existing and still dreamed of, to improve and further humanize the employee experience?

I would suggest posing some of the following questions:

- Does the technology do what it promises?
- Is the thing it promises beneficial to multiple parties (e.g., employees, the company)?

- Is the technology truly easy to use?
- Is the technology an intuitive, all-in-one-package experience, or does it require multiple platforms, log-ins, training sessions, refresher courses, and so on?
- Is there a non-tech way to do almost exactly what the tech does?
- Does the tech have too many exceptions to the rule?
- Is the tech truly customizable?
- Can the tech be used in other settings?
- When users find problems with the tech or want features added, does it take a long time to implement those improvements?
- Whom does the tech leave behind?
- Who benefits most by using the tech? Is it the one who made it? Are their values your values?
- When conceiving of the tech, did the developer think first of an audience to satisfy or a skill to automate?
- Was the tech created with empathy?
- When all is done, is the experience that the tech automates or simplifies a genuinely positive one?
- What questions haven't been asked here that you should be asking?

A Bad Use of Tech

Asking questions beforehand and all throughout the process – and afterward, too – is good business, and humane. The lure of developing technology can be so seductive that the developer or purveyor can't see the forest for the trees. My colleague, Dr. Steve Hunt, shares a good example.

For years, says Steve, there has been a steady increase in the use of employee self-service technology solutions. These solutions allow employees to complete administrative HR, IT, travel, and procurement tasks instead of having them completed by support professionals. This includes things like requesting vacation time, enrolling in benefits, transferring employees, filing expenses, accessing tax forms, changing job titles, adjusting pay levels, posting job openings, and myriad other activities associated with the administrative side of work. Good idea, right?

Maybe, but maybe not.

Rather than paraphrase the idea, I asked Steve if I could reprint a passage he wrote on the topic, titled "Stupid, Ineffective, and Cruel"[6]:

There are two major advantages to self-service solutions. First, they allow companies to save workforce costs by eliminating support services roles. Second, they provide employees with the ability to perform tasks independently. This can create a greater sense of efficiency and autonomy. However, this second advantage is predicated on the assumption that self-service solutions are effective. Sadly, all too often this is not the case. What is even more sad is that many companies are unaware or insensitive to the pain, frustration, and suffering that bad self-service technology is inflicting on their employees.

Empirical research has shown the negative impact that bad technology experiences have on employees. These solutions do more than just frustrate employees. Ineffective self-service solutions send a message that the company does not appreciate employees' time. Consider the results from one survey that asked employees whether their company's HR self-service solutions made them feel "undervalued, ineffective, empowered or impactful." Thirteen percent of the employees said undervalued; 40 percent said ineffective. Roughly one-third of employees also reported being "irritated" and "frustrated" by self-service solutions that were supposed to make their jobs easier! Several of the solutions had been deployed for years and tolerated under the illusion of administrative efficiency.

Forcing employees to use bad self-service solutions is . . .

Stupid. The hourly rate of managers and line employees is usually higher than the rate of administrative support staff. Many self-service systems require employees to struggle at completing unfamiliar tasks that could be done by experienced administrative staff personnel in much less time. It does not make financial sense to have employees complete administrative tasks unless it takes considerably less time than having them done by lower-paid administrative staff. This is not the case with many self-service solutions.

Ineffective. When self-service systems are poorly designed, employees will try to minimize time spent in the solution. This includes purposefully leaving out or changing information to make the process faster. For example, a manager might reclassify an employee turnover reason from involuntary to voluntary to avoid going through additional steps that might be forced upon him or her if he or she provided the real reason why an employee left the company. The result is a solution that systematically creates bad data.

Cruel. Self-service solutions often support tasks that employees must complete to move forward with their work (e.g., get a new computer, hire a staff member, complete expenses, adjust an employee's pay). Forcing employees to use poorly designed self-service solutions to perform these tasks can create considerable stress and anxiety. Many employees openly admit to having sworn or lost their tempers due to bad experiences with self-service technology. Companies are requiring employees to use systems that literally raise their blood pressure.

The problem with self-service solutions is not the idea of employee self-service. It's forcing employees to use poorly designed solutions. Many companies' self-service solutions use legacy on-premise platforms that cannot be easily accessed using mobile technology. They also use outdated user interfaces and contain HR and financial information that is unfamiliar to most employees. This is a result of how these solutions were designed. Rather than building a true self-service solution, companies took old legacy solutions designed to be used by support professionals and changed them so that managers and employees could login to them directly. Or they designed self-service solutions based on what the support functions need them to do, not what employees want them to do. As a result, many employees are forced to use self-service solutions that were never actually designed for them.

To be truly effective, self-service solutions must be designed so employees find them simple to use. This starts with using mobile-enabled solutions updates with modern user interfaces. These systems should leverage the same sorts of artificially intelligent interfaces found in consumer platforms that employees use outside of work. Companies should also be sensitive to asking employees to do something that is not what they were hired to do. It is financially inefficient and culturally disrespectful to require professionals hired for their specialized skills to spend significant time on tasks that could be performed by administrative support staff. Start measuring how employees feel about the experience of using self-service technology. Do not simply ask them if it is easy to use; also ask them whether they feel it is an appropriate and effective use of their time.

A recent study by managed services company ADP found that one of the biggest factors affecting whether employees like their HR department was having an HR person they could talk to in person who they knew by name.[7]

Steve has a clever solution to keep poor self-service technology from happening, a fix that "provides insight into how much a company's senior leaders truly appreciate the value of their employees' time." Steve's fix requires executives to use the same self-service solutions they expect their employees to use. And to make sure they do it getting the same level of administrative support their employees receive.

Then see what happens.

The Digital Employee Experience

Tech solutions should do exactly that – offer solutions to problems. But sometimes they create more problems (while possibly also solving the original one). Employees don't care if the experience or process is owned by HR or Procurement or IT. They just want it to be seamless and always available.

As your company creates or refines tech for a better employee experience, remember that the true outcome – the employee's wish, the last bit of the last mile – needs to be delivery of the promise. It doesn't matter how cool the process is if it doesn't work. For example: You discovered a new ride-sharing app. It looks slick and appealing. But it turns out it's difficult to log into. Also, the car doesn't show up. We would all agree that it is *not* a good experience, no matter how colorful the graphics might be.

Companies that are designing or imagining the next part of their enhanced employee experience program should bring employees into the process. Find out how to make it flexible, intuitive, people-centric. Empower their people with an intuitive design. Find out what matters to them most, what will deliver true value, and what will delight them!

A better digital experience is vital in the actual work the employee is doing, and could mean the difference in the company's survival. A few years ago, a very big industrial customer of SAP's was struggling due to a downturn in its relevant markets, which pummeled their revenue. They recognized the need to digitally transform; they went from what they had been to a technology player. They overhauled their offerings, as well as their manufacturing facilities. They transformed the office experience, which significantly influences employee experience. They acquired some startups in the San Francisco Bay Area to capture the tech talent they needed to make their pivot. They reduced some of their traditional workforce at the manufacturing sites and increased their reliance on contingent labor.

They ran into a bit of a problem, though. As they onboarded this new tech talent, they began to realize that the end-to-end employee experience, along with the digital component, was lackluster. At the time, one industry survey found that more than a third of employees reported that they would leave their current employer for an organization that offered a more digitally progressive experience, and I know that the number has gone up since then. (We all know people who've done that: One of my colleagues quit a job because he had to use Lotus Notes instead of Microsoft Outlook and had to do his expense reports manually.) Our client's CEO saw that they weren't going to retain this tech talent unless they improved their tools – and that led to a significant purchase, which allowed them to transform their end-to-end digital employee experience, a key part of their business objective of digitally transforming.

Where's the Off Switch?

Employees may know when to step away from technology to live their best lives and experience their whole selves.

But that doesn't mean that tech will step away from them.

Over the course of the pandemic, more than 25 percent of companies purchased technology to "passively track and monitor their employees," even as many firms had yet to figure out how to balance employee privacy and the company's ultimate goal (whatever it may be). Less than half of surveyed employees trust their organization with the data being collected on them; nearly half receive no information about the data. While regulations are expected to limit what employers can do, that remains a concern.[8]

And it's not so easy for the conscientious individual to step back in the first place. "From a mental health perspective, I think it goes both ways," says Claudia, a PR executive. "Technology is great, with so many different platforms to help you streamline your work. You can compartmentalize your work communication on Slack. You can have multiple Google calendars. But the double-edged sword is that your life and your thinking are now owned. Technology is everywhere. You can't ever leave it. I can turn off Slack notifications on my phone but I'm just going to have anxiety the next morning when I see that I missed ten notifications. There is no off switch. Oh, I have two minutes to myself while walking from this meeting room to the next? Nope, actually I have zero time, because everything is scheduled on a block and everyone knows you're in front of your computer. No travel time required."

Do we know the net effect of all this technology – on productivity, on relationships, on peace of mind? To be honest, not really. More companies deploy, according to Deloitte, "analytics solutions to predict retention, correlating factors such as compensation, travel schedule, manager, and demographics to understand why certain people are less engaged than others." And what have they found? Not much that's conclusive. "High-technology companies . . . throw benefits at employees to see which ones stick – unlimited vacation, free food, health clubs, parties, stock options, and fun offices are common. Do these all result in high engagement? Most companies can't really tell you."[9]

I remember when I spent a high school semester in Germany as a foreign exchange student. No phone, no email, no internet, few English speakers. The things that kept me going were the handwritten letters I received from my family, schoolmates, and hometown neighbors. I'm not suggesting we go back to snail mail. But the challenge with every new form of digital communication is to find a way to personalize it, to make it your own, so that you come through to the other person. Even if your company's employee experience is being created ultimately to make things more efficient, to streamline, to reduce boring and repetitive tasks, to speed things up: It was created by a person. It was created for a person. Together, those two people, or the two circles they're part of, can find a way to keep some of the humanity intact. The part that matters.

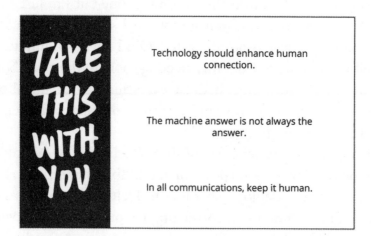

TAKE THIS WITH YOU

Technology should enhance human connection.

The machine answer is not always the answer.

In all communications, keep it human.

CHAPTER

9

Thriving at Work
A Focus on Health

I f your house was on fire, and assuming every living creature in it was safely out, what's the one thing you would grab on your way out?

One of my favorite teachers, Bill Lawson, posed that question to us in our 11th grade Humanities class, and of course it got all of us thinking – a bunch of 17-year-olds starting to consider big issues and the wider world.

But such a question makes anyone think, at any age. It challenges you to consider hard what matters – what *really* matters, when you're asked to make sacrifices.

As long as people have been working, they've been asking this question: *Is work worth it?*

Today, there is a greater number of people than ever pondering the question. Employees are facing a growing list of challenges that are causing them to take a hard look at work: a historic misalignment in the U.S. labor market, the unprecedented number of people quitting jobs and not immediately looking for other ones, the pandemic and its aftermath and the economic and social toll they have taken. All of these point to an existential crisis for so many – employees, future employees, ex-employees – about the way most of us spend most of our waking hours.

It's not hard for work to overwhelm us. For all the good intentions of leaders to make the employee experience positive and balanced, for many workers, including the most skilled, their job essentially starts the moment they wake up. It continues when they get home, since they're continuing to check emails, texts, Slack, and so on, throughout what remains of their evening. Sometimes, the tendency to get overwhelmed rests with the individual: It's just how you're wired. Some of it is the culture of the company you work for. Some of it, as I wrote, is the larger culture. Some of it is the industry. Emma, a physical therapist and yoga instructor, works to help people with back, neck, and other body misalignment issues. She says she's had success with all kinds of people except one. "I get these young execs coming in, guys in their late twenties, who work a hundred hours a week, lots of it sitting at a computer, and their backs and bodies are all messed up. They come to my studio and ask me, 'What can I do in 15 minutes to make it better?' I tell them there's nothing. They would have to take their situation and their bodies more seriously and make some changes to get aligned and get to less pain. But they look at me like I told them they had to grow another head."

We won't manage the changes we're going through right now at work without adjusting the way we approach work itself, any more than someone can fix 100 hours a week of bad posture with 15 minutes of yoga.

Mind, Body, and Spirit

Our quality of life is directly linked to our ability to maintain healthy boundaries. If your work experience is a cycle of reaching a stressed-out breaking point, taking time off, and then continuing to be overworked, burnout is inevitable. This cycle will continue unless there is an intentional shift.

Many employees today are evaluating what they're getting out of their work experience and what they're giving up. Is it worth it? They're looking at their whole self, not just the "part" that goes to work separate from the parts that do everything else.

The whole self framework affirms that the present matters and the future matters; that your health – physical, mental, emotional, spiritual – is crucial in both the present and the future. It cannot be neglected or trivialized. Your dreams can become real only if you're doing something today that moves you in that direction.

In recent years, we've started to focus more on the total health and well-being of the employee. Why?

- The pandemic provided us with a renewed understanding of the importance of holistic well-being. First, it forced organizations to prioritize the physical well-being of employees and customers, shifting well-being from benefit to business imperative. Then it became clear that the impacts of the pandemic stretched far beyond just physical health, with more employees experiencing more stressors today than arguably ever before.

- The boundary between life and work, dwindling for years, completely dissolved in 2020, and now employees and companies are trying to decide how they will continue to embrace this hybrid dynamic; leaders are considering if and how much they will encourage employees to return to the office.

- Workforce well-being strategies have expanded beyond traditional benefits to company-wide initiatives. Examples include building aspects of culture that focus on fitness and nutrition, meditation, and mental wellness activities, as well as a focus on modeling general well-being. The data show that these companies are attracting better talent and producing better results.

Many aspects of life need to be addressed to make us feel whole. For too long we thought we could "silo" life, but we can't. If we could, we wouldn't have the phrase "work-life balance." "The expectations of the workforce have changed for the better," says Jen Fisher, Chief Well-Being Officer of Deloitte US. "People are saying, 'Look, I don't want to sacrifice everything for my job and my career.'"[1]

We know so much more today about the elements of good health, brain health, general well-being, and how to achieve them. Thanks to science and access to educational resources on a range of health-related topics, we are seeing the connections:

- Meditation can improve brain health.
- Working out can relieve the negative impacts of stress.
- Healthy eating has an immediate impact on our alertness and processing.
- Sleep is vital to being at our best at work as well as in our interactions and relationships.
- Professionals should address mental health issues when needed.

If we connect these things with what we know about the importance of task experience, social experience, and fulfillment experience – the three basic types of employee experience – then a great experience is reliant on good health.

Let's start with mental health.

Toward Better Mental Health

On October 10, 2021, I greeted a colleague on a conference call with, "Happy Mental Health Day!"

There was a pause. Then she said, "Great, so in that case, there's something I'd like to share before we kick off this call . . . I'm not sure I took my meds this morning. So I might be a little bit erratic."

She laughed and said her comment was partly in jest, but that she was also glad she could communicate something as candid and real. "I don't think I ever thought I would volunteer to the president of my company, 'Hey, I'm not sure I'm medicated for my attention deficit disorder this morning.'"

At my company, we're getting better at allowing people to be themselves, to feel psychologically safe. Nothing about the employee experience is more crucial, or has gained prominence faster, than valuing employee mental health.

All health matters, of course. Lots of people, physically fatigued from so many obligations, would prefer to work fewer hours. They want more flexibility to work out and stay physically fit. Numerous employers are offering expanded parental leave. Workers and companies alike want office environments that are pleasant, that make it easier to take a break, eat healthy, and enjoy overall wellness. A physical environment that solves for this is increasingly a must-have, not a nice-to-have. A smart company has an inviting office with comfortable chairs and good natural light not because it makes a good impression but, first and foremost, because it helps with employee well-being.

Despite all the adjustments that companies make, burnout is a massive problem, nationally and internationally. Nearly 80 percent of U.S. workers are concerned about their mental health as burnout skyrockets.[2] And it's not just because of the pandemic. "Of the nearly eight in 10 workers concerned about their mental health, 77 percent cited stress and burnout as the biggest challenges . . . the major factor for the worsening condition is an increasing workload with half saying work demands are taking a larger toll than COVID-19."[3] Columnist and author Arianna Huffington calls out "this delusion that burnout is the price you must pay for success."[4] Social scientist and author Arthur Brooks refers to "success addiction."[5]

If companies want their employees to have an acceptable experience, if they wish to retain their top talent, then they need to address the dangers of burnout. Their people expect and demand it. Three in five employees say they'd "feel more motivated and more likely to recommend their organization as a good place to work if their employer took action to support mental well-being."[6] And almost nine in ten workers, according to a survey by the American Psychological Association, finds that workers "at companies that support well-being initiatives are more likely to recommend their company as a good place to work."[7]

While a good start, initiatives and programs designed to combat stress – e.g., mindfulness, healthy eating, and exercise – are not enough to prevent high levels of burnout in today's environment. A bigger lever is the work itself. Managers should partner with Human Resources to monitor demand level and find a balance.[8]

With data and analytics, companies can do more to help shift and ease the load that employees carry. This will improve their health, including mental health, and lead to more productive employees and better business outcomes.

We still don't talk about mental health the way we do physical health, but we are trending in the right direction. For me, mental health has always been important, but never as much as going for a run or eating my vegetables. Living in Texas, you can imagine how much effort both of those activities take.

Today, we are faced with increased feelings of anxiety, loneliness, "languishing," and burnout – health indicators that aren't mainstream but should be. If we don't talk about these issues now and address them head-on, the mental health crisis – for employers and the wider world – will only worsen.

Toward Better Physical Health

Taking care of our physical health can be overwhelming. It's important for companies to support the physical well-being of employees if they expect them to have long, productive, fulfilling careers.

The basics of good physical health include simple elements like eating right and regular exercise, as well as having proper access to health care and benefits.

"For me personally, my company gives me the flexibility to take care of myself," says Sammy, a financial analyst. "If I don't have to commute, then I have the ability to work out in the morning and meditate. Not every day is the same, so being able to fit in my workout whenever it makes most sense is really important." That kind of flexibility and empowerment helps employees improve how they perform the rest of the day.

Peloton has done considerable research and taken this idea to the next level. They offer companies the opportunity to provide employees access to classes along with motivating features that build community, benefiting employees and the overall business. Peloton says that 64 percent of their members felt more productive at work.[9]

Another employee recently shared her more critical situation. She said, "I took a job as a security guard because of the health benefits. Since I'm pregnant, my top priority was a reliable benefits package. Then a new firm took over my company and the new management threatened to reduce my benefits. I was so scared."

It is crucial to understand each employee's unique health situation, so that even in times of change, the company can preserve trust as well as the physical health of its people.

Doing Your Part

Just as companies leverage data and insights to gain a holistic view of their customers, employers seek the same of their employees. They want to build curated experiences that are meaningful for employees, allowing them to bring their best to the workplace and ultimately become more productive. Companies want to understand their workforce at a more detailed level but must be careful to maintain their privacy and not infringe on personal data. Conversely, employees *want* to share their information in the pursuit of a better experience, especially when it comes to health and benefits. Alight's 2019 Health and Financial Wellbeing Mindset Study found that up to 70 percent of workers say that they are comfortable sharing personal health information with their employers in return for personalized guidance in managing their health.[10] (In Chapter 5, I discussed the difficulties that companies can have in getting personal information from employees; when workers know exactly what and who the data are for, they are more likely to share.)

Before the pandemic, many employees would have loved a gym in their office, right? It's a common perk that many saw as critical, or even came to expect. A mid-size financial company was considering building an on-site gym at their new office but the price tag was high. They had partnered with their benefits provider and reviewed pages of market research that portrayed an office gym as the ultimate way to achieve corporate wellness. After a quick survey, they discovered that only a small fraction of their employees had an interest in working out at the office. The employees mostly preferred the flexibility to drop into an out-of-office spin class or meet their friend for a trail run. And the *last* thing they wanted was to run into a client, sweaty after an office workout. By gathering feedback and insight (however personal), the company found that vouchers or stipends for a local gym would be a much more meaningful offering for their employees – better-used and more cost-efficient.

The data are clear: Employees who are healthy are more productive. Companies with healthier, more productive employees are more innovative and successful.

How can a company do its part in helping employees get to better health? Some ideas to consider:

- Companies can sponsor meal plans and healthy snacks in the office.

- Leaders can make time for employees to share their own practices for good health (both recognizing and empowering more of the same).

- Companies can sponsor fitness competitions and collaboration around steps, cycling, or yoga participation.

- Leaders can help share information and educate their teams on healthy habits.

A focus on employee health extends well beyond physical health. Often, addressing physical health has compounding effects on mental, emotional, and even spiritual health.

Sarita shared her story about the unexpected benefits of a company wellness initiative. Sarita lives in Chiang Mai, a large city in northern Thailand. In her role as a marketing expert, she is the only one on her Southeast Asia team located in Thailand, and often felt lonely, even isolated from her peers. A few years ago, her company introduced "Race to Rome," a Fitbit challenge to walk hundreds of thousands of virtual steps from Asia to Italy. The goal was to boost healthy habits and encourage employees to prioritize exercise. Each team had to log their steps as a group and share and track updates along the way. Her team went all in, logging steps, going on virtual walks together, and cheering each other on over WhatsApp. They were quickly the #1 team in the company. Though it was a small initiative (with a completely different goal), for the first time she felt connected to her team. They finally had something in common besides work.

A great employee experience isn't about the perks or offerings. It's about how people *feel* when they come to work, including their health. Physical, mental, emotional, and spiritual well-being all contribute to the sustainability of the workforce and, ultimately, the business.

A foundation of great employee experience
is great employee health.

Health is more than physical. It's emotional,
mental, and spiritual, as well.

You can't recover from a 100-hour work
week with 15 minutes of yoga.

IV

So What?

Only you can control your future.

Dr. Seuss

CHAPTER 10

The Results Are In
Productivity and Effectiveness

It's an open secret that certain types of businesses are designed to maximize the money you spend there. Casinos might be the most well-known and openly manipulative examples: no clocks or windows, so you lose track of time. Free drinks, if you're gambling. Ambiguity about where the casino actually begins and ends. Grocery stores also exploit human psychology. In fact, casino design was considered so successful in achieving its goals that many of its principles were adopted by grocery stores. The "essentials" – milk, bread, eggs – are placed at some distance from each other so you have to make your way down other aisles, increasing the chance you'll spot nonessentials to throw in your cart. Fresh produce is often near the entrance so you'll select some healthy food early and, feeling virtuous, be likelier to reward yourself with items you might not have considered. They've come up with a formula that works.

What does this have to do with employee experience?

Although today's world is more transparent than the past, there are still some unspoken rules about what makes people more productive and more effective – and it's not psychologically manipulative for companies to promote conditions that do this, when it's good for them *and* the employee. Perhaps it's the equivalent of organizations getting their people to eat broccoli.

So: What are the conditions that make people work best?

The biggest motivators for employees – presuming fair compensation, safe working conditions, and a sense of stability – are purpose, meaning, connection; belonging and a sense of being recognized and valued; agency and autonomy.

When employees feel a sense of psychological safety, *they perform well*.

When employees are in good physical and mental health, and not on the verge of burnout, *they perform well.*

When employees work in environments that are inclusive and diverse, exposing them to new perspectives and different ways of solving problems, making for both a richer work experience and personal experience, *they perform well.*

When employees are led well, *they perform well.*

When employees' whole selves are cultivated, *they perform well.*

When employees have the right tools, *they perform well.*

I talk with people about employee experience all the time. I discuss it with all kinds of people, in all kinds of settings – with my own teams, in virtual global meetings of thousands, in discussions with our customers, on business-focused podcasts. In most cases the people I talk to are deeply engaged in the discussion. It strikes so close to home for them, as it does for all of us. It's about the place we spend more waking hours than anyplace but home, often even more than home. It's about people we work side by side with, for hours every workday, often for years, and who get to know us and whom we get to know, for better or worse. It's about the driving, exciting purpose (if we're lucky) that we devote so much of our physical and psychological and intellectual selves to. Our experience at work affects so much of what we do *outside* of work, the topic of how we feel *at* work could hardly be more relevant. So most people I talk to want to talk about it right back with me. And we are all focused on making it better.

Of course, some think that improving employee experience is a fad, something that will go away soon, and the next business management idea will take its place. Some think: *It really doesn't affect the bottom line.*

But it does.

If your company is known for providing better employee experiences than the competitor across the street, talented individuals looking for their next job will find out easily which company has the better culture, can provide them with the best opportunities for learning and career growth, and will deliver a more pleasant day-to-day experience. If your company has not made employee experience a priority, it won't be a secret for long. Not in today's connected, wired, social-mediated, global village of a world. That should be reason enough to elevate your employee experience: You're limiting your pool of talent, including high performers.

Making better employee experiences is one of the main ways you future-proof your company. Because when you have a workforce that's happy and engaged, they will crush the obstacles in their way. When you have an engaged workforce that's operating with psychological safety, they can *see* the obstacles to their productivity. They feel confident in their abilities. They know they can take risks and offer bold ideas because if they fail, it's okay, and they will be supported in finding another way. If employees have line of sight to the customer, it propels them to deliver faster and better. When you have software developers who understand and have empathy for the end user, they are likely to deliver more effectively. When there's purpose, then managers who want to lead well can articulate that vision in a way that the team trusts and believes. They can see where they're going. A purposeful, happier, healthier workforce doesn't mistake activity for impact. If employees understand the purpose, then they understand what they're trying to achieve and want to achieve; they know the meaningless activity to cut out. They're connected to their purpose. They see the vision. They know they're playing a vital, valued part in turning it into reality, along with members of their company, their unit, their team. My son, Cole, is an offensive lineman on his high school football team, and he and his fellow linemen do what they do – block the defense from getting to the quarterback, clear lanes for the running backs – because they see the goal line. They have a shared purpose to get there. Simple.

When a business leader establishes a great work culture, providing employees with the opportunity for a superior experience, the reward is not merely a "Wow, this is great. Nice place to work." It's the loyalty and productivity of a determined, grateful, effective workforce.

Better employee experience leads to better productivity. Simple. This is supported by research. As I mentioned at the beginning of this book, the Thrive XM 2020 Index demonstrated a clear correlation between employee experience and financial performance.[1]

Thrive XM 2020 Index

🌱 16 percent year-over-year growth
(average growth for top 20 companies)

📈 Improved Fortune 500 rank by 11 places
(average growth for top 10 companies)

$ Every ThriveXM point equates to an added
US$53 per employee in revenue

I began this chapter writing about ways that casinos and groceries accomplish what they want to do as businesses: Create circumstances that make their customers buy more, whether it's potato chips or poker chips.

Creating a superior employee experience – one with a clear sense of vision and purpose – is one of the most significant things you can do to attract and retain happy customers.

Different People, Different Styles

I want to distinguish "efficient" and "effective."

The first term means to get the thing done quickly, without waste; the *how* of the action stands out.

The second term means to get the thing done that you intended, without question; the *what* of the action stands out.

Very often these terms are used one for the other but they're not interchangeable. If there's something you need to do and you do it efficiently, that may or may not be a good thing (e.g., you may do it but without heart, without passion, without understanding the point). If you do something effectively, then you did it in a convincing, satisfying way; the one thing we can't tell from such a description is how you did it.

The how is up to you.

Everyone has their own style, needs, and preferred working conditions. Hemingway wrote standing up, starting early in the morning. Edith Wharton wrote in bed. Kurt Vonnegut took frequent breaks for pushups and sit-ups in between writing. Kafka didn't start writing until late at night. Understand the particulars of your employees, give them the freedom to create their preferred environment, then let them do their thing so they can be their most productive selves. Some people work best on their own, others in collaboration. Today, leaders are wrestling with issues around remote working, and whether it's wise and productive to have every employee come back to the office, just some people, alternating days, those workers who want to, and so on.

"I can't believe how many unproductive hours I spent in traffic," says Avi, now at a firm that's walking distance from his home. "If I was doing it now, I would be listening to Audible, books on tape, but either way, I wasn't doing anything that was helping the customer or the company. I saw it as a lost hour and a half four days a week, two and a half hours on Friday, which was brutal."

While I can't say I miss all the commuting I once did, I used it to charge up or power down, and both were necessary grace periods to make me the best I could be at work and at home with my family. True, except for the occasional call in the car, I wasn't using that time directly to benefit the customer, but without it I would have been less helpful and productive overall.

"It's crazy to think that you need people in an office full-time to be productive," scoffs Avi.

Everyone's different – but it's a good bet that when you treat employees with compassion and understanding, and they treat each other that way, you will have more productive workers. Research shows that when company leadership supports its workers in their personal lives, those employees tend to "perform at a higher level."[2]

Gordon, a senior executive, starts all of his initial one-on-ones with these ground rules. "We're not going to talk about a business problem. We're not going to talk about anything related to work. I want to know who you are. Tell me about what drives you. Tell me about your family. Tell me about things you like to do." While he will adjust the circumstances around each employee's working environment as he gets to know them better, he feels that this first encounter builds trust, caring, and openness. This introduction means that when they *do* have a business problem (to take an example), it won't fester the way it otherwise might, meaning they will be more productive. "If they have something personal on their mind that's affecting their work, then they're more likely to feel they can tell me," he says. "I need to know that as a manager."

Says Leila, an executive, simply: "People are more effective at work when they're happy. I'm not an animal person but some people can sit there with their cat on their lap while they're writing code, or just knowing their kids (who can sometimes be a distraction) are in the backyard – that takes so much stress away and allows them to focus more. There are times when you're collaborating or on deadline when you can't control all the conditions. But I say you should work when it works for you to work."

At Forbes.com, Jason Wingard writes that "any newly remote culture should emphasize communication and connection."[3] Trust matters, too: Two in five remote employees, according to a Gartner study, want more self-directed work. "Managers must trust their employees and shift away from directing their work to coaching them to success," the study concludes. "To do this, managers should focus on employees' work product and outputs rather than processes."[4] Remote work is great for the self-starters among us, maybe not so much for those who need more structure.

We now have technology that enables more choice in when, where, and how we work – but today's workers are often most interested in the what and why of it. That comes down to values, not the strength of a WiFi connection. If leaders can accommodate some of the values and personal tendencies of each worker, then they are helping a team to perform effectively and productively. And most importantly, happily.

Does the same concept that applies to employee preferences also apply to managers? Well, managers are often the accommodators, the reflectors of what they think the worker most needs to be effective and productive. As a manager, maybe you're not the cheerleading type – but you could be more vocal than you might be naturally, if that's what your direct report needs. Maybe you're completely hands-off, which works well for employees who prefer that – but what about the ones who need more guidance? It's on the manager to make some sort of shift. They obviously need to work in a way that's authentic, but a leader also needs to read the situation and the person and show empathy to deliver the best results.

Productivity is what you get when you deliver a clear purpose for your business, empower agency and autonomy for your employees, create a culture of belonging, and actively show that you value your people.

Never Mistake Activity for Impact

"I feel most effective when I'm busy and I think a lot of people feel that way," says Ethan, a salesperson.

I don't doubt that's true.

David, also in sales, recounts, "When I first started this job, you could mistake activity for achievement. I worked really hard all day, every day, and for a long time didn't really move the needle finding real opportunities, in closing, in making a real impact on customers. Was I effective? I guess not."

I might balance his assessment with this: He's become a very successful salesperson, and presumably some of the knowledge he uses today was learned back in those "unproductive" and "ineffective" days early in his career.

With certain jobs, activity *does* equal achievement: when it's a pure numbers game and your job is to pack as many boxes as possible, knock on a certain number of doors, or count widgets.

"Being busy is great," concludes David. "Being productive is better."

Keeping busy when you're burned out is inefficient *and* ineffective. "Engaged people need *time to think, create, and rest*," a Deloitte survey reports. "At Google, the policy is called '20 percent time': a day a week set aside to work on something new or outside your normal job function."[5]

Lourdes, who works as a freelance designer, says of her main client, "I don't have access to paid time off because I'm not a full-time employee there. If something comes up and I can't get something done on schedule, though, I can just share the situation honestly, and they're good about it. Everyone on the team works really hard. They've established a culture where everyone is all hands on deck, and everybody wants to do well and trusts others are doing their best, too."

The company, the industry, and the national culture can also make hard workers feel as if they're "never working hard enough, never doing it quick enough, never doing enough, period," says Rebecca, when that's not necessarily the case.

Peak productivity happens when the individual is equipped to make the effort – and that includes possessing the proper state of mind, bank of energy (physical and mental), and intention. Jim Loehr, world-renowned performance psychologist, says, "Time is an opportunity that becomes valuable only in its intersection with energy and becomes priceless in its intersection with extraordinary energy . . . it's not how long we spend at work, how much time we spent with our family, how many dinners you were home for, but rather the energy you brought to the time you had."[6]

An employee experience that focuses on purpose and a sense of belonging and recognizing value is naturally more productive. It allows people to focus on the impact they are making with their time and energy. They will never fall victim to mistaking activity for impact, because the focus is clear.

Crushing the Obstacles

No matter how sharp the worker, a faulty system can slow down everything.

Robert tells the story of someone he knew who graduated from college and went to interview for a sales position with a Fortune 500 company. They gave him a test. He failed it. He was rejected for the position.

It happened that his parents knew someone at the company, so the company decided to hire him anyway. He went on to become the #1 salesperson for the whole organization.

Clearly, something in their assessment approach was wrong. How many other amazing salespeople had they failed to hire because of their supposedly conclusive test? To their credit, they reevaluated the test and their approach to hiring (at least for salespeople). They recognized that qualities like great interaction with individuals, along with the ability to work well in a team, far outpaced whatever their test was meant to evaluate.

My daughter, Kalie, a college sophomore, was recently going through a gauntlet of job interviews right now. Her major is International Studies, with a focus on commerce; she's doing in-depth study of the forces of economics and global business models. She has lived in Asia, has excellent grades, and is involved in multiple campus leadership roles, like the Student Government Executive Committee and the Academic Affairs Committee. (Do I sound like a mama bear?) Recently, she was turned away from a management consulting firm. I understand that. Every company has its own approach and needs. But the reason they gave for rejecting her was that they were not hiring for her major. Another company that passed on her told her that they had already filled the roles at her preferred office location.

I point this out not to lament the difficulty Kalie experienced in landing a job. She accepted a great offer at another firm. I point it out because far too many companies, when doing some of their most critical tasks – including assessing new skills and hiring talent – act against their best interest or take an approach that is woefully outdated. In today's world, does an office location even matter? You may have a herd of thoroughbreds, running as fast and effectively as they possibly can, but if the track is muddy and you've done nothing to improve it, they won't get where they're going very quickly.

One of the best salespeople I know was frustrated because he had taken the unconventional path, and his promotions, recognition, and compensation had suffered for it. Now, taking stock, he comments, "I regret not climbing the traditional ladder. A role opened up that I should have been considered the ideal candidate for, but the decision-makers didn't see me like that. I should have 'de-risked' my résumé by going through the traditional hierarchy. Should it matter that I was overseeing every customer-facing resource? It should, but it doesn't. My last year as a salesperson, as an individual contributor, I sold more by myself than any first-level sales manager globally. So I became very defensive and arrogant in the interview. I hadn't checked all the skill-set boxes I needed to, and they basically told me 'it would be good if you did that.' The amazing thing is that what I was already doing was so much more complex than these boxes I had to go and check. They needed me to be more qualified on paper than I was in real life."

Each of these stories features a major flaw in recruiting, hiring, and assessing great talent. These are obstacles to productivity. With a healthy culture and employees who strive for a growth mindset, you can identify and address these obstacles and flaws in the system.

Productivity from Anywhere

While employees and their leaders will find ways to create peak working conditions that yield optimal productivity, the Human Resources department will be key in creating the best mix. Amanda Rajkumar of Adidas has said, "HR . . . we are the ombudsman between employer and employee. We are the conscience of the firm."[7] This is especially true in the era of increased remote/hybrid work, where HR must manage what amounts to a massive experiment in employee productivity. Will it work? Will it be better? Will it be harder to measure if it's working? HR will need to adjust compensation and benefits as employees relocate and talent strategies turn borderless. New learning, especially in the form of one-on-one mentoring, will be necessary to fill the skills gap.[8]

Will productivity be measurable? Yes – but we may need to zoom out. Research has found that "what remote workers gain in productivity, they often miss in harder-to-measure benefits like creativity and innovative thinking."[9] Studies find that workers sharing a room tend to solve problems more quickly than remote collaborators.[10]

Studies show that productivity and creativity go hand in hand. And creativity may require a little serendipity, often a result of chance meetings that come from working in the same space. Steve Jobs, a huge proponent of in-office work, said, "Creativity comes from spontaneous meetings, from random discussions. . . . You run into someone, you ask what they're doing, you say 'Wow,' and soon you're cooking up all sorts of ideas."[11]

Different environments work better for different people. And different types of work require different environments. Some people find the commute a waste of time while others find it productive in allowing for downtime and recharging. Some people can work through the night and actually thrive doing so, while others must be in bed by a certain hour to be their best selves for the day. Leaders have many things to manage and oversee, including the harmonious and productive work of individuals, maybe a team of them. To the extent that a leader can empower each worker to find their most effective natural style, everyone wins.

Leaders must focus on the things that are proven to make a difference. Empowering workers to find new ways to capture creativity, shedding obstacles and old ways of thinking, and directing Cheir energy at the tasks that are meaningful and impactful: That's a key to great employee experience and a productive organization.

* * *

I love that there is always more than one way to look at things, if you're open minded.

It's worth stopping now and then to refresh in your mind what certain terms mean to you. Earlier in the chapter, I made a distinction between "efficiency" and "effectiveness." Well, what does it mean to be "productive"? What does the word *productive really* mean? I thought I had a pretty good idea before I spent a semester in Spain as a college student. For the first time I was confronted with the concept of siesta – how, at two in the afternoon every day, you would leave your school or job, go home, have a meal with your family, maybe watch TV, maybe take a nap. It felt shockingly countercultural to an American girl. Suddenly, I was surrounded by people who had a very different approach to getting things done. The Spanish stopped what they were doing at a peak part of the day and didn't really emerge again until four or five in the afternoon, sometimes as late as six, when everybody went outside to shop and engage with each other and finish the day. Engagement, but on a completely different timescale. I wrote my dad a letter describing it, and when I got home I was eager to tell him more. I was certain he would be appalled.

He wasn't.

"Maybe that's how it should be," my dad said. "Maybe they've got it figured out and that's how you're really more productive.

After all, life is a marathon, not a sprint." No judgment from him, just admiration. I was expecting someone born and bred in Texas would say, "Oh, those lazy people, they don't know what work is!"

Instead, he was impressed. "Maybe that's something we could learn from," he said.

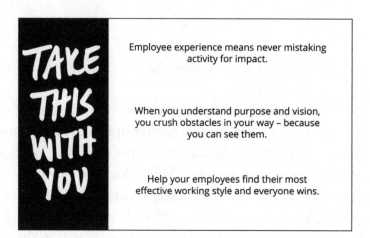

TAKE THIS WITH YOU

Employee experience means never mistaking activity for impact.

When you understand purpose and vision, you crush obstacles in your way – because you can see them.

Help your employees find their most effective working style and everyone wins.

Keep the Pace
Agility and Resilience

The title of Part IV of this book – So What? – is a little brasher than the others.

Why?

It's not meant to be dismissive. It's meant to respond to those who might question the impact of employee experience, on everything from an individual's happiness to a company's collective morale to the bottom line.

But that two-word question also seems appropriate because it separates out the value of employee experience in the present and in the future. *Yes, employee experience may help my company right this moment, but so what? Is it really going to matter down the road?* The whole self model I've discussed is about who we are now and who we are tomorrow, about being *and* becoming. This chapter addresses those who might believe that improving employee experience is a short-term fix, for the present and maybe the near future, and not necessarily beyond that.

Predictions are almost guaranteed to fail. But I believe that when a business commits to better employee experience, it is planting a flag (*Here is a set of rules for our company's culture*) that positions it well for the future. Why? Because a company that is serious about culture is engaging in a form of organizational behavior change. That shows ambition. You don't make that kind of investment unless you're looking down the road. A change that focuses on enriching the employee experience enables *agility*, which, along with technology and continuous learning, better prepares you to keep pace with ever-evolving market change.

Even the definitions of recently trending learning terms – upskilling (providing training to employees to improve performance in their current roles) and reskilling (training employees to take on a completely new position, particularly when business objectives have changed) – speak to a mindset that must toggle between present-thinking and future-thinking.

- Agility is the ability to quickly shift business models. This is made possible by upskilling and reskilling quickly.

- An employee culture that includes a growth mindset prioritizes learning; learning drives agility.

- Resilient employees weather difficulties better and create a sustainable culture for times of crisis.

So a focus on employee experience delivers results beyond just talent attraction and retention. It makes your business more agile and resilient.

Companies are waging a talent war, aggressively recruiting candidates with the same or similar skill sets. For some jobs, it might be cheaper, faster, and more effective to train existing employees to perform at a higher level – or in an entirely new role. But it's not an either-or proposition. It's essential to couple effective recruitment with a learning and development strategy, since investing in your workforce improves retention, productivity, and innovation.

A Learning Culture

COVID-19 profoundly disrupted business. Certain industries saw demand skyrocket while others bottomed out, companies were forced to navigate ever-changing protocols, and many workers traded their desk for the dinner table. Numerous organizations proved nimble and responsive. If companies can effectively transition overnight, then something at their very foundation served them well.

That sounds like a learning culture.

Though they may not have this on thesaurus.com (they don't; I checked), a synonym for "learning" is "empowering." Those who know more have a greater ability to help customers, colleagues, companies – and themselves. According to a Deloitte survey, "Learning opportunities, professional development, and career progression are among the top drivers of employee satisfaction. Employees under the age of 25 rate professional development as their number one driver of engagement, and this is the number two priority for workers up to age 35."[1] People crave learning.

Agile and resilient employees create agile and resilient companies. Another reason why today's skilled workers crave learning: the economic landscape demands it. Today, a higher level of preparation is required for an increasing number of occupations. According to Pew Research, in 1980, the number of U.S. jobs that called for "average to above-average education, training, and experience" – everything from electrician to lawyer – was virtually identical (actually, slightly below) to those requiring "below-average education, training, and experience." By 2015, the former group topped the latter by almost 20 million. Simply said, far more of our present workforce needs significant preparation. That means a minimum of an associate degree or equivalent level of vocational training; prior job experience; or one to two years of formal or informal on-the-job training. Jobs calling for average or above-average levels of social skills (e.g., interpersonal, communications, management skills) nearly doubled in the same 35-year period; jobs requiring greater analytical skills (e.g., critical thinking, computer use) rose more than 75 percent. Jobs in these latter two categories include nurses, post-secondary teachers, civil engineers, and chief executives. Jobs requiring greater physical skills (e.g., machinery operation, technical and electrical work, etc.), such as carpenters and welders, rose a mere 18 percent, even as "overall employment in the economy increased 50 percent" in that time span.[2]

Unsurprisingly, when compared to their competitors, organizations with a strong learning culture are more productive and profitable, and their employees are more likely to be engaged and to stay with their companies.[3]

Traditionally, companies have favored performance cultures to learning cultures. Adam Grant has said that a performance culture has a chilling effect on behaviors that lead to success. "In performance cultures, the emphasis on results often undermines psychological safety. When we see people get punished for failures and mistakes, we become worried about proving our competence and protecting our careers. We learn to engage in self-limiting behavior, biting our tongue rather than voicing questions and concerns. In performance cultures, we also censor ourselves in the presence of experts who seem to know all the answers – especially if we lack confidence in our own expertise."[4]

What's a learning culture? It's founded on curiosity. To foster such a culture, managers pose thoughtful questions to employees, opening lines of communication and creating space for employees to provide feedback without fear of reprisal.[5]

These cultures cultivate different mindsets. "Employees in a performance culture ask: Will this be on the test; will I get a bonus; can I put this on my résumé? . . . While employees in a learning culture ask: How does that work? Will this teach me something new? I wonder what would happen if . . . ?"[6]

A learning culture is more essential than ever. Employees need to pick up new skills or shift to different areas within the company to adapt to market demands. They also need to learn how to abide by new safety protocols or transition processes for remote environments. When hiring slows, companies need to identify what skills already exist within their workforce so that they can optimize their talent. That affinity for learning breeds resilience.

Leaders need to reinvent their companies as next-generation learning organizations to win in the next decade.

- The more opportunities people have to learn relevant skills for their jobs, the happier and more productive they'll be.[7]
- Today's process of learning via formal classroom education, then working, then retiring will be replaced by a new pattern that will extend for decades: learn, work, break, learn, work, break.[8]
- 86 percent of respondents to Deloitte's 2019 Global Human Capital Survey cited learning as an important or very important issue, the number-one concern, more than human experience[!], leadership, talent mobility, and rewards.[9]
- As the working world and the products companies produce become increasingly digital, the skills present in a company's workforce, as well as the traits of its workers, will be their biggest competitive advantage. The same goes for their leadership. Increasingly, a company's assets are intangible.

A learning culture cultivates agility. Many of SAP's customers use employee profiles to take inventory of their current skill sets. For example, one large health care organization conducted an impromptu inventory of employee skills so that they could better match the urgent requirements in the field. This enabled them to quickly redeploy talent, giving them flexibility in a time of critical need.

Would such a mix-and-match of an organization's workforce make it more productive? Would it help leaders identify talented workers who may be slotted in the wrong roles or loaded with the wrong responsibilities, and relocate them to positions where they can better realize their potential? This type of talent mobility is becoming more common, even expected, and it benefits employees and businesses alike.

Every Learner Is Different

What is your employee's preferred learning style? Learning on their own, one-on-one, or in a group setting? Is it visual, auditory, reading, writing, kinesthetic? Does it call for more communication or more engagement of a different sort? How do you manage the difference between knowledge workers and frontline workers? Is the learning intensive or spaced out over time? Is it formal or informal?

One manager in Asia described how his team learns most effectively with "more focused learning. Gone are the ways we used to learn – you know, two days of learning an overly general Managers Managing Managers program, and, boom, I'm a certified manager. Focusing in on a very specific area – operational excellence, business processor dimension, etc. – is brilliant. My people like continuity, practice, and a dose of technology."

A company that honors employee experience also honors training and learning; you can't do the former without also doing the latter. Learning is essential for future-proofing. It builds more capable individuals, and stronger, more cohesive teams – hallmarks of agility and resilience. The more skills the employee develops, the more capable and adaptable they become.

The possibilities for developing as a learning organization are many, varied, and exciting – not to mention profitable. Does the company provide hands-on training? Does it provide free content up to and including premium learning labs? Does it develop its own learning ecosystem or use education consultants and partners?

However a company chooses to deliver personalized learning and development programs to upskill and cross-skill its team, the effort starts with an accurate assessment of where things are now, identifying gaps in knowledge or skill set. After the leader establishes an understanding of the current skills landscape, the company can offer training and education tailored to both the business priorities and the learning styles on the team. Follow that with meaningful one-on-one coaching and track progress.

Here's broadly what leaders want to accomplish:

- Assess employee needs and skills gaps.
- Enable virtual learning that targets skills to match employees' new priorities. Use collaboration tools to support social learning.
- Link learning items directly to goals (performance or development).
- Provide ongoing coaching and feedback.

Creating the space for learning is challenging. It's one of the first priorities to get shoved to the side, especially when budgets are tight. One study showed that the typical employee had 14 free minutes for training. Not per day. Per *week*.[10] Further, leaders must make sure that any upskilling or reskilling plan aligns with a broader, strategic workforce plan.

Learning is more than a one-time event. It needs to be continuous, readily available, and requires a workforce that's open to developing new skills. Upskilling is a key factor in the long-term stability and growth of an organization. Employee learning and development, like employee experience, directly impacts business results. A commitment to upskilling and reskilling signifies that businesses care about competing now and are invested in long-term success.

Resilience

During my semester abroad in college, I took the train to Switzerland. I wanted to try skiing the Swiss Alps.

It's important to understand that I was not much of a skier. In my life up to that point, I had lived in Texas and only once skied the slopes of the mountains near Taos, New Mexico. There's a reason there's never been an Olympic gold medal skier from Texas.

My lack of skill didn't stop me. I made my way to the famous ski resort town of Zermatt. Fearlessly and foolishly, I took a gondola and ascended the world-renowned mountain, watching in growing concern and finally horror as the landscape became visible below me, *way* steeper and scarier than I had imagined. Way more than I was prepared for.

At the top of the run, alone, not equipped with the language skills to ask for help, I felt stranded. But help arrived, in the form of two veteran skiers, old Swiss guys who looked like they could do these runs in their sleep. They guided me down, pointing the way through the rocks and trees, until I found myself actually enjoying the experience. With ready courage and some unexpected mentorship, I learned what I needed to learn, just in time.

No broken bones. Or broken spirit. In fact, I was soaring.

Was it dumb? Maybe. Am I sorry I did it? Of course not!

Sometimes an employee should take a risk even when they're not ready for it. Business leaders are guiding their organizations through a new reality. Workers, many with increased and changing responsibilities, are finding the courage and skills they need to adapt.

Work that challenges you is a great draw for many. When Chara was interested in moving to a leadership position in her corporate office, she pegged her readiness at "about three years." Resolved, she went to her manager to share her plan.

"Why three years?" her manager asked. "Why not one?"

Chara was terrified at the idea of moving up that fast – and yet, within the year she had become a manager and was soon enough thriving in the role, as if she was made for it. She appreciated being pushed "beyond my limits. I had been doing extremely well there but I knew I had a lot more potential." She is happy with her company because "they always see growth." Her previous employers didn't bother to push her.

People do well when there's a chance of reward but also when there's some risk; the thrill of *I don't know how I'm going to succeed, but I know that I can and I'm up to the challenge.* Stakes are important. Stakes make you care.

Lack of new challenge results in lack of growth. Employees should always ask, "What's next for me?" If not, then their managers should be asking them, or encouraging them to think about it.

Employees, many of them with increased and shifting responsibilities, are learning. A key is the support of others: When we're out over our skis, but someone is there to support and help us, we go from surviving to thriving. Companies need to stretch their employees but also support them. This continued cycle of challenge and skill-enhancing also builds resilience.

How, exactly, do companies "build" resilient employees? By engaging them with a personalized employee experience that helps them meet and exceed expectations in work and in life. In today's world of disruption, a resilient workforce will help the organization navigate uncertainty and continue to grow.

* * *

People talk often about the future of work. In fact, as I was preparing to write this book, I considered writing about just that. The future of companies. The future of organizations. The future of work itself.

I realized that by focusing instead on employee experience, I could touch on things that have as much to say about the future of work as anything. Companies with a great employee experience are the companies that are performing well.

The same may be said of training, skilling, and learning: Look to see which companies have a learning culture and are successfully engaging their employees, and you are sure to find many of the winning companies of tomorrow.

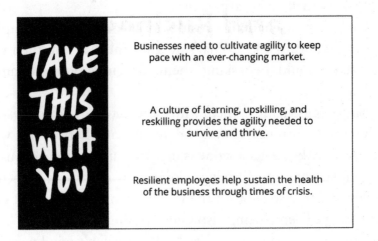

TAKE THIS WITH YOU

Businesses need to cultivate agility to keep pace with an ever-changing market.

A culture of learning, upskilling, and reskilling provides the agility needed to survive and thrive.

Resilient employees help sustain the health of the business through times of crisis.

Sustainable Growth for People *and* Business

By this point I hope I've made a persuasive case for the importance and numerous benefits of positive employee experience – in the lives of workers themselves, the people they work with and for, and the companies that employ them.

I hope I have made a case for the authentic leadership, ingenuity, and empathy that business leaders must exhibit to establish or improve on an organizational culture that elevates employee experience.

Employee experience will help us *achieve a more sustainable world* as we deliver on important people metrics.

The world is confronting so many evolving challenges. It can be hard at times to get a coherent view of it all, much less to have a set of coherent solutions. One of my joys around employee experience – thinking about it, implementing programs that honor it, reviewing data and anecdotal evidence to help our customers and our teams refine and improve it – is that it's a lens through which we view other relevant issues. I don't think it's overstating the importance of employee experience to tie it to the three ambitious points at the start of this chapter: how it helps us to relate to each other; how it helps us to spread the benefit to others; and how it helps us to get a little closer to a path that is sustainable.

These are all epic points. Employee experience has something to say about all of them.

All Voices Should Be Heard

For all of our vast differences, the foundational idea behind employee experience – greater empowerment for people – is one that can be felt by more than just the segment of high-performing, highly skilled workers. "There are some general things about how people feel about other people that I still believe are universal," says Mark, who spent years overseas in Asia and Australia. "Do you trust them? Do you care about them? Are you interested in them as a person, no matter where you are? Sure, you may not do well shouting in Japan. Or saying anything negative in Thailand. Or being timid or overly formal in Australia. That affects how you conduct business and negotiate contracts. But when you get outside of the conference room, everyone cares about the same thing." My South African-born colleague, Frances Botha, who has worked all over the world and set foot in over 90 countries, says, "People are more the same than they are different. Everyone wants to feel a sense of belonging. Everyone wants to feel that they're doing a good job. Everyone wants appreciation. Everyone wants to feel personal security and psychological safety. The difference is in how we want it."

This is a laboratory experiment. All ideas and all voices should be heard. The more we hear each other's voices and learn from the Chinese perspective, the Brazilian perspective, the American perspective, the Spanish perspective, the Nigerian perspective, the more we learn from each other, the more relevant we can be in this globally dynamic environment. We've been doing so much more in a virtual setting since the early months of 2020. In some ways it has allowed for a more level playing field, a more frequent window into each other's lives (and living rooms). It's a more multifaceted conversation, yet one where we see that many of us want the same thing – more dignity, more security, more freedom. Tsedal Neeley writes that "team leaders, whether they serve mostly international or local markets, must develop Global Leadership Aptitude. This aptitude demands that you learn to develop panoramic awareness, actively frame the situation, and exercise the capacity to act immediately."[1] She also writes, "Global teams have to ensure that the fluent English speakers learn to dial down dominance, the nonfluent speakers learn to dial up engagement, and everyone, especially the managers, learns to balance for inclusion."[2]

Now we're starting to leave that laboratory and return to our previous work lives, or some version of them. Painful as this period has been, it has also been, says one worker, "super-motivating, very energizing . . . like in college where you stay up all night, ordering pizza, working hard to prepare for your presentation the next day. Those were formative experiences. This feels like one of those."

Yes, our circumstances and cultures are different. There are generational differences. But technology, greater access to information, and communication, taken together, provide a level of intimacy and shared experience unlike anything any of us has ever witnessed. It allows for continual learning on a broad scale. We're actually coming much closer to speaking a common language. Neeley, once more: "Learning to trust and connect with one another virtually is even more effective if combined with direct knowledge about the personal characteristics and behavioral norms of far-flung virtual colleagues. When remote teamwork includes periodic face-to-face meetings we can make conscious efforts to learn about other people's lives rather than jumping immediately into a prescribed work agenda."[3]

The goal is to have more people enjoy a positive employee experience. But that's an empty goal without some engine driving forward. That engine? The people who are right now expecting and even demanding more from their work experience. The values that increasingly drive *them* – a greater sense of purpose, meaning, connection, the belief that all of us have value – can help bring the world closer.

Expanding the Tent

It's a little harder to be a barista from home.

Or a nurse. Or an EMS worker. Or a pharmacist. Or a truck driver, food delivery worker, police officer, firefighter. Or countless frontline jobs, and many knowledge jobs, too. Only about one in four U.S. jobs can be done remotely.[4]

Lots of workers across the globe might not feel part of this conversation, whether they ply their trade in Maine or Moscow or Mongolia.

"There are many positions that don't have the freedom of choice I have," says one knowledge worker who has the "luxury of flexibility" and "hasn't been in an office in eighteen months." He says, graciously and correctly, "That lack of choice is probably true for the majority of workers in the world."

Says another fairly senior employee who was able to work remotely during the first year-plus of the pandemic, "Money isn't everything – when you're making pretty good money."

A colleague recently told me that she was conversing with one of our customers in Asia – a conglomerate that counts a hotel chain and various food-related chains in its empire. "I was talking about the 'rich employee experience' and how we could put our system in place for all of their employees, and they could then pull all this useful information," she recounted. "The customer said, 'We have several thousand employees in our chain of bakeries and we barely know those people's names.' The client said, 'We train them in an hour, then they go bake cupcakes or whatever we need them to bake. If they show up for work, great. If they don't show up, we get somebody else.'" It will be a long time before many of the issues in this book reach those workers. The idea of finding a company that cares about their experience might seem quaint, or not even compute.

The luxury of choice is something still unavailable to many. There are those who had to get a job straight out of high school. Or maybe they left college before getting their degree because they had to work. Or they have second and third jobs because they need to make ends meet. Many people lack any real financial support network. They find themselves in a soul-crushing job where they don't feel as if they have the option to make any changes without disruption to their health care and savings. There are people working jobs that make them feel continually unsafe and, worse, don't feel as if they can demand changes or quit until something better comes along. A few years ago, Thomas Kochan, co-director of the MIT Institute for Work and Employment Research, noted, "There's an erosion of the employment relationship. Companies are focusing on their core competencies and paying attention only to their most talented workers, and then subcontract out the rest without worrying about the employment conditions in those areas. That's a big issue."[5]

The creed of employee experience will be heard differently in different countries. In some, workers generally don't expect much change without a shift in government policy. In others, women are far behind men in having any sense of control over their work conditions, and would never ask for fair pay or a better experience. And in some countries today, LGBTQ+ individuals wouldn't dream of pressing for certain occupational benefits or wishes.

Even within the same country, the understanding of employee experience can differ wildly. When I lived in Singapore, I had to occasionally travel to Japan, where I was introduced to *omotenashi*, the tea ceremony central to Japanese culture. It means "to wholeheartedly look after, or serve, guests" and consists of an exquisite, open appreciation of the simplicity and beauty of everything around you. On the other hand, Japan's business culture has given birth to a relatively new word, *karoshi*, which means "to work oneself to death." It is not the only country that contains such contradictions about one's basic experience of the world.

Employee experience will be heard differently in different industries. Some professions remain male-dominated, especially at the top, and it may be a long while before women feel the luxury of choice and any ability to grow their career.

People who live in rural areas may feel they have far less flexibility in their job possibilities versus their urban counterparts.

Subcontractors, freelance workers, part-time workers, gig workers, adjunct professors, waiters, dishwashers, employees without benefits may feel that employee experience is exclusively for the full-time salaried worker. Or maybe not. "When I think of my employers, there are just so many, like a hundred different people a year," says Nate, a non-unionized, freelance, very busy lighting operator in film and TV, "but I have the same concerns as any employee."

There are winners and there are losers, as there always are during times of great change. We hope that the promise of new technology and a continuing evolution of human values will mean that the number of winners will go up, and the number of losers will go down. It doesn't have to be a zero-sum game.

Recently, we've seen restaurant workers collaborate with customers to advocate for sustainable food practices, but now we're also seeing them advocate together for good working conditions. There's a growing interest in the workforce itself to operate together in new ways. Increased employee listening and corporate action on the issues that matter could help to create a safety net that provides health care, workplace safety, and access to savings, all of which make a huge difference in the daily life of workers.

We all want purpose, agency, recognition, and belonging. As we focus holistically on these critical elements of employee experience, we create a better environment for more workers everywhere.

Achieving People Sustainability

The World Economic Forum provides metrics on three areas of "people sustainability"[6]:

- *Dignity and Equality*, which focuses on providing equitable opportunities to all employees in recruitment and selection, training, development, and promotion . . . in a workplace where all employees feel valued and respected and receive fair treatment with appropriate compensation and benefits. By embracing diversity and equal opportunities, companies can help integrate underrepresented groups and minorities into the labor market, so they become a better reflection of society and also deepen the pool of talent that a more diverse workforce can bring. It looks at measures such as pay gap, living wage, discrimination and harassment incidents, collective bargaining, and more.

- *Health and Well-being*, which focuses on the expectation that organizations care for the health of employees and their families and to uphold their rights to adequate physical and mental well-being. . . . Companies that maintain high standards in health, safety, and labor rights can see higher levels of employee productivity and operational efficiency. It looks at measures such as monetized impacts of work-related incidents, workers' access to non-occupational medical and health care services, and more.

- *Skills for the Future*, which focuses on access to skilled workers . . . addressing the skills-gap challenge, companies must increase investment in training, educating, and reskilling their workforce to grasp the opportunities of changing work patterns and workplaces due to new tools and technologies. It looks at measures such as average hours of training per person, number of unfilled skill positions, increased earning capacity as a result of training, and more.

With greater transparency and focus on these metrics, we'll drive the behaviors and actions for a more sustainable future.

Leading the Way in Employee Experience

Many of today's most successful companies understand the importance of employee experience, and in some cases have for a long time. They deliver impressive growth in part by focusing on their workers and delivering a unique, powerful, superior employee experience.

Starbucks: We all love a great – and personalized – cup of coffee. As a Starbucks customer, you get a consistent product, made just for you, fast. It's clear that their culture was designed to care for employees; satisfied employees are at the heart of the customer experience, and in turn their strong global growth.

Starbucks:

- fosters a culture of fun and community among its employees
- realized that the greatest costs – stores that lost revenue – were those without managers; regular succession planning then helped to reduce, and almost eliminate, lost revenue due to manager turnover
- takes care of employees with benefits, because they want you, the customer, to get more than a great cup of coffee

The company's stated mission is "to inspire and nurture the human spirit – one person, one cup, one neighborhood at a time." They also say, "We are performance driven, through the lens of humanity." Their belief in people extends beyond the customer to the employee (and the community). Starbucks founder Howard Schultz has said, "You can't expect your employees to exceed the expectations of your customers if you don't exceed the employees' expectations of management."[7]

Singapore Airlines: If you've ever flown with them, then you know the quality experience on the island-nation's flagship is unlike any other. Named among the world's best in air travel year after year, the airline offers a unique experience peppered with details and surprises (champagne on arrival, delicious multi-course meals, endless entertainment options), yet consistently delivers exceptional service across every class. What might be some reasons for this?

Singapore Airlines:

- focuses on support for employees through benefits and travel experiences
- centers their "people strategy" on the promise of learning and development opportunities
- enables that ever-elusive "work-life balance" – as noted repeatedly, for example, in reviews on employer review site Glassdoor

Is it a surprise that this great flying experience is made possible by proud employees dedicated to their purpose?

Adidas: Their products and brand inspire athletes across the globe – world-class, aspiring, and weekend – enough to make them the top sporting goods manufacturer in Europe, and second in the world.

Adidas:

- is led by their purpose: "Through sport, we have the power to change lives"

- is focused on diversity and inclusion
- is driven by the 3 C's of confidence, collaboration, and creativity

At the Adidas headquarters in Herzogenaurach, Germany, there are employees from 100+ countries. Employee resource groups create networks to give a voice to workers from different walks of life.

These companies and others like them are not sitting still. They know that their employees and future employees are in a state of constant progress and evolution. With these changing needs and wants, an organization's leaders must continually review and address how to engage and care for them. They know that building a strong employee-first culture takes time, effort, and ingenuity.

Creating great customer experiences is something that smart companies do. For companies looking to continue sustainable growth, creating great employee experiences is something they must also do.

One of the reasons both employers and employees pay attention to Glassdoor is because it collects anonymous evaluations from workers and candidates. As a worldwide leader on information about jobs and companies, it offers insights into the employee experience powered by millions of ratings and reviews. According to Glassdoor, the following companies are creating great employee experiences, which explains their appeal to job-seekers around the world:

- Bain and Company: "They've put forth a very thoughtful COVID response plan and upped their game on DE&I in the wake of recent events."

- In-n-Out Burger: "Amazing people, awesome leadership, I feel cared about every single day and we make the best burgers on the planet."
- Johnson & Johnson: "Many opportunities in various departments, welcoming and friendly environment, and work-life balance."
- Microsoft: "Good work/life balance, teamwork, great culture, flexibility to pursue my intellectual goals and challenge my potential."
- REI: "Management is supportive and understanding, they give great consideration for time-off requests."

* * *

Employee experience matters. Companies must realize that there is a way to deliver it without spending millions of dollars or waiting years for a total technology transformation. Leaders can start right now, and along the journey see real improvements in productivity, agility, and resilience – for the workforce and the business.

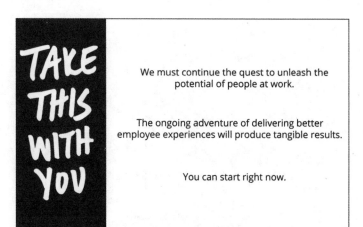

TAKE THIS WITH YOU

We must continue the quest to unleash the potential of people at work.

The ongoing adventure of delivering better employee experiences will produce tangible results.

You can start right now.

Epilogue

Storm Home

In school, one of my favorite teachers introduced our class to Garrison Keillor's concept of a storm home. It's a place – physical or otherwise – where you can go when your life feels surrounded by difficulties and challenges. When you're caught in the rain, struggling to deal with stress or trauma, or if you're just having a bad day, it's a place where you can feel safe. People can be part of your storm home. Anyone who helps you feel safe and whole and hopeful can contribute to your storm home. We all need a storm home at times – when we feel overwhelmed by stress and uncertainty, or when we lose hope.

There have been times in my life when work served as my storm home. After my father's death, I was sad and overwhelmed with loss. Friends encouraged me to take time away to grieve and recover. However, it was work that supplied the structure I so badly needed. Work prevented my mind from a spiral of negative thoughts. It challenged me and offered respite from the loneliness I felt after his passing. I had support from my family at home, but work provided something else. When your experience as an employee is positive, your job becomes much more than a paycheck. Recognition, a sense of accomplishment, community, added purpose, even sanctuary – that's what work *can* be.

In an age of doubt and mistrust, where people have lost faith or confidence in core institutions, one's job and workplace can bring a welcome sense of purpose and meaning. This is a critical moment for leaders to examine what's genuinely beneficial for the worker and the organization – and what's not. *Perhaps my single greatest motivation for writing this book is to argue that what is good for the company can never again be separated from what is good for its workers.*

Work is always changing. In the 1920s, the most common job in America was dairy farming. By the 1980s, it was secretarial work; 30 years later, it's retail.[1] What constituted work in 1870 looked far different from a 40-hour week in a 20th-century factory. What about a 60-hour week in an office today? Is work better now? By how much?

It's a challenge, of course, because not all industries (or companies or jobs) are created equal. But I would contend that things have changed for the better. Technology has taken over the most tedious tasks. Access to continuous learning is far greater. Companies that take effective advantage of the technology and platforms available can develop their people like never before. The dreadful and often lethal working conditions of years past have been eliminated or significantly improved in many industries and parts of the world (though by no means all). The expectations of leadership have broadened. Vulnerability is no longer considered a weakness, but a strength. Authenticity matters more than perfection.

I'm not trying to paint an unrealistically rosy picture of work today and in the near future. I know that there are dying industries. Jobs are disappearing. Certain skills are fast becoming obsolete. There will be workers who are left behind. Creative destruction is required to move ahead, and globalization is great, but also incredibly complicated. If we are to be constructive about what lies ahead, then we need to be as honest about what we have lost as what we have gained. The late cultural critic, Neil Postman, author of *Amusing Ourselves to Death*, noted that every time we adopt a new technology, we make a Faustian bargain: Something is gained, and something is also lost. The telephone allowed us to connect with others far away like never before, but also altered our notions of intimacy and privacy. The automobile made the world smaller, shortening distances so that travels that took weeks now took mere hours, but it also hurt air quality, choked our cities, and degraded the beauty of our natural landscape. The same scrutiny can and should be applied to the computer, the internet, the smartphone. The modern-day organization and office, as with all innovations, brought with it consequences that were good (e.g., connection, access to mentors, brainstorming) and not so good (e.g., inequity, burnout, sedentary conditions).

Once entrenched, society acted as if these new facts and behaviors were sacred and unchangeable. They're not, though. Many of these beliefs and behaviors are dogmatic and dated, doing as much harm as good – to the individual employee, to the business, to the larger society.

What have we lost that we might want to restore?

Consider "death by spreadsheet." Any tech or businessperson will have heard it, and probably used it. It means to have your productivity and decision-making overwhelmed and eventually undermined by data, the very thing you thought would *help* productivity and decision-making. It suggests that analytics are driving every decision, even those that it shouldn't.

Don't get me wrong – I love analytics. Numbers give you guidance and identify trends. They help determine what customers are buying and how they're using your products;

which markets are expanding, and which are contracting; and inform decision-making and future strategies. I would not be where I am today without a genuine appreciation for analytics.

As we move toward a more human-centered work experience, we must trust in people and their capabilities, their ability to work together, and some qualities that can't be captured in a spreadsheet or database. Human understanding, relationships, and connection are cornerstones, not afterthoughts.

Is it unrealistic to wonder about the business impact of everyone caring about each other a little more? It costs nothing. It produces actual results – greater collaboration, a willingness to go the extra mile, a reduction of fear and the courage to try new things. It fosters the psychologically safe environment employees have come to expect.

All this requires leaders who empower their employees. Deloitte's Jen Fisher believes that "everybody should be the Chief Well-Being Officer of their own life." She also says, "We have extensive evidence that when leaders who empower and who have achieved success talk about the things that are hard, it makes it easier for everyone else to do it because they realize that it's not a sign of weakness."[2]

Business leaders must never forget what a good working environment can do for people. When that work is dignified, challenging, and connected to purpose, it allows individuals to become a better version of themselves.

Leaders can future-proof their company by focusing on employee experience. Work is not a place to get wrung out so that we have nothing left for our real home. To make work *work* – be it the literal, physical space or the cultural spirit – leaders must remember that work is a virtual home. It's a place of learning and growth, community and connection, meaning and purpose and value.

A business that is invested in the people who make it go, appreciating each and every person's whole self: That's a place we all want to be.

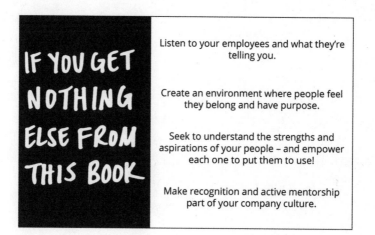

IF YOU GET NOTHING ELSE FROM THIS BOOK

Listen to your employees and what they're telling you.

Create an environment where people feel they belong and have purpose.

Seek to understand the strengths and aspirations of your people – and empower each one to put them to use!

Make recognition and active mentorship part of your company culture.

Notes

Chapter 1: A Brief, Not Particularly Employee-Friendly History of Work

1. Emma Goldberg, "In a 'Workers Economy,' Who Really Holds the Cards?" *The New York Times*, November 3, 2021, nytimes .com/2021/11/03/business/jobs-workers-economy.html
2. Paul Krugman, "Is the Great Resignation a Great Rethink?" *The New York Times*, November 5, 2021, nytimes.com/2021/11/05/ opinion/great-resignation-quit-job.html
3. Tom Kalil and Farnam Jahanian, "Computer Sciencs is for Everyone!" Obama White House blog, December 11, 2013, obamawhitehouse.archives.gov/blog/2013/12/11/computer-science-everyone
4. Annette LaPrade, Janet Mertens, Tanya Moore, and Amy Wright, "The Enterprise Guide to Closing the Skills Gap," IBM Insitute for Business Value, ibm.com/downloads/cas/epymnbja
5. "Calculating Migration Expectancy Using ACS Data," United States Census Bureau, census.gov/topics/population/migration/ guidance/calculating-migration-expectancy.html
6. Jesse Noyes, "7 Big Statistics About the State of Flexible Work Arrangements," Workest by Zenefits, July 11, 2018, zenefits.com/ workest/7-big-statistics-about-the-state-of-flexible-work-arrangements/

7. "Artificial Intelligence in 2019: Getting Past the Adoption Tipping Point," Blumberg Capital, August 1, 2019, blumbergcapital.com/ai-in-2019/

8. "The Future of Jobs and Skills," World Economic Forum, 2016, reports.weforum.org/future-of-jobs-2016/chapter-1-the-future-of-jobs-and-skills

9. "2017-2018 State of Enterprise Work Report," Workfront, 2017-18, workfront.com/resources/2017-2018-state-of-enterprise-work-report-u-s-edition

10. Moore's Law.

Chapter 2: Employee Experience: The New Why

1. Maria Figueroa Kupcu, "Taking a Stance," Brunswick Group, June 4, 2019, brunswickgroup.com/social-issues-ceo-response-i14995/

2. Ibid.

3. Dan Pontefract, "Yet Another Survey That Demonstrates Employees Want Purpose But Organizations Are Not Delivering," Forbes .com, June 9, 2016, forbes.com/sites/danpontefract/2016/06/09/yet-another-survey-that-demonstrates-employees-want-purpose-but-organizations-are-not-delivering

4. "The Business Case for Purpose," *Harvard Business Review*, assets. ey.com/content/dam/ey-sites/ey-com/en_gl/topics/digital/ey-the-business-case-for-purpose.pdf

5. Gary Burnison, "Breaking Boredom: What's Really Driving Job Seekers in 2018," Korn Ferry, kornferry.com/insights/this-week-in-leadership/job-hunting-2018-boredom

6. Melanie Baravik, "5 Surprising Employee Development Statistics You Should Know," Clear Company, September 9, 2021, blog. clearcompany.com/5-surprising-employee-development-statistics-you-dont-know

7. "2019 Workplace Learning Report," Linkedin Learning, learning. linkedin.com/content/dam/me/business/en-us/amp/learning-solutions/images/workplace-learning-report-2019/pdf/workplace-learning-report-2019.pdf

8. "The Future of Work Arrives Early," Oxford Economics, Society for the Human Resources Management, and SAP SuccessFactors, shrm.org/hr-today/trends-and-forecasting/research-and-surveys/documents/sap%20oe%20shrm%20global%20report.pdf

9. Jodi Kantor, Karen Weise, and Grace Ashford, "Inside Amazon's Worst Human Resources Problem," *The New York Times*, November 3, 2012, nytimes.com/2021/10/24/technology/amazon-employee-leave-errors.html

10. Owen Hughes, "Tech Workers Warned They Were Going to Quit: Now, the problem is spiraling out of control," ZDNet, October 22, 2021, zdnet.com/article/tech-workers-warned-they-were-going-to-quit-now-the-problem-is-spiralling-out-of-control/

11. "Quotations on the Jefferson Memorial," Monticello.org, monticello.org/site/research-and-collections/quotations-jefferson-memorial#footnote10_ytmztxy

12. "World GDP per Capita, 190-2021," Macrotrends, macrotrends.net/countries/WLD/world/gdp-per-capita

13. Farhad Manjoo, "Even with a Dream Job, You Can Be Antiwork," *The New York Times*, October 22, 2021, nytimes.com/2021/10/22/opinion/work-resignations-covid.html

14. "Business Roundtable Redefines the Purpose of a Corporation to Promote 'An Economy That Serves All Americans,'" Business Roundtable, August 19, 2019, businessroundtable.org/business-roundtable-redefines-the-purpose-of-a-corporation-to-promote-an-economy-that-serves-all-americans

15. World Economic Forum and Willis Towers Watson, 2020.

16. Jeanne Meister, "Employee Experience Is More Important Than Ever During the COVID-19 Pandemic," Forbes.com, June 8 2020, forbes.com/sites/jeannemeister/2020/06/08/employee-experience-is-more-important-than-ever-during-the-covid-19-pandemic/

17. Qualtrics XM Institute.

18. Lewis Garrad and Thomas Chamorro-Premuzic, "How to Make Work More Meaningful for Your Team," *Harvard Business Review*, August 9, 2017, hbr.org/2017/08/how-to-make-work-more-meaningful-for-your-team

19. Jill Popelka, "Thrive XM Index 2020 Report: The Case for Employee Experience Driving Business Results," SAP, October 7, 2020, news.sap.com/2020/10/thrive-xm-study-2020-employee-experience-business-results/

Chapter 3: More Than a Job: Purpose, Meaning, Connection

1. Michael F. Steger and Bryan J. Dik, "Work as Meaning: Individual and Organizational Benefits of Engaging in Meaningful Work," August 2012, michaelfsteger.com/wp-content/uploads/2012/08/Steger-Dik-HPPW-in-press.pdf
2. Richard Lederer, "Our Last Names Reveal Alot about Our Labor Days," *The San Diego Union-Tribune*, September 5, 2015, sandiegouniontribune.com/sdut-last-names-english-language-lederer-2015sep05-story.html
3. Steger and Dik, "Work as Meaning."
4. Ibid.; Hardy, 1990; Schuurman, 2004.
5. Ibid.
6. "3/4 of Millennials Would Take a Pay Cut to Work for a Socially Responsible Company," Sustainable Brands, November 2, 2016, sustainablebrands.com/read/organizational-change/3-4-of-millennials-would-take-a-pay-cut-to-work-for-a-socially-responsible-company
7. Frank Brietling, Julia Dhar, Ruth Ebeling, and Deborah Lovich, "6 Strategies to Boost Retention Through the Great Resignation," *Harvard Business Review*, November 15, 2021, hbr.org/2021/11/6-strategies-to-boost-retention-through-the-great-resignation
8. "Becoming Irresistible: A New Model for Employee Engagement," *Deloitte Review*, Issue 16, January 27, 2015, www2.deloitte.com/us/en/insights/deloitte-review/issue-16/employee-engagement-strategies.html
9. Adam M. Grant, "Outsource Inspiration," faculty.wharton.upenn.edu/wp-content/uploads/2013/12/Grant_OutsourceInspiration.pdf

Chapter 4: You Got This: Agency and Autonomy

1. Facebook page for Lagom HR, facebook.com/LagomHR/photos/ a.824523241260367/1171095443269810

2. "Workplace Learning Report," LinkedIn Learning, 2021, learning .linkedin.com/content/dam/me/business/en-us/amp/learning-solutions/images/wlr21/pdf/LinkedIn-Learning_Workplace-Learning-Report-2021-EN-1.pdf

3. Roy Maurer, "Internal Marketplaces Are the Future of Talent Management," SHRM, April 16, 2021, shrm.org/resourcesandtools/ hr-topics/talent-acquisition/pages/internal-marketplaces-future-of-talent-management.aspx

4. Jane E. Dutton and Amy Wrzesniewski, "What Job Crafting Looks Like," *Harvard Business Review*, March 12, 2020, hbr.org/2020/03/ what-job-crafting-looks-like

5. Ibid.

6. Brian Kropp, "9 Trends That Will Shape Work in 2021 and Beyond," *Harvard Business Review*, January 14, 2021, hbr.org/2021/01/9-trends-that-will-shape-work-in-2021-and-beyond

7. Ward Williams, "Countries Offering Digital Nomad Visas," Investopedia, July 15, 2021, investopedia.com/countries-offering-digital-nomad-visas-5190861

8. Sergio Ocampo, "Countries That Will Pay You to Move There," MoveBuddha, May 17, 2021, movebuddha.com/blog/countries-will-pay-you-to-move-there/

Chapter 5: We Belong: Progress on Diversity, Equity, and Inclusion

1. "Becoming Irresistible: A New Model for Employee Engagement," *Deloitte Review*, Issue 16, January 27, 2015, www2.deloitte.com/ us/en/insights/deloitte-review/issue-16/employee-engagement-strategies.html

2. Josh Bersin, "Why Diversity and Inclusion Has Become a Business Priority," JoshBersin.com, March 16, 2019, joshbersin. com/2015/12/why-diversity-and-inclusion-will-be-a-top-priority-for-2016/

3. Julia Taylor Kennedy and Pooja Jain-Link, "The Power of Belonging: What It Is and Why It Matters in Today's Workplace," *Coqual*, 2020, page 2, coqual.org/wp-content/uploads/2020/09/Coqual PowerOfBelongingKeyFindings090720.pdf

4. Amanda Rajkumar speaks with Adam Grant on podcast, "Introducing Forward," news.sap.com/2021/10/introducing-sap-original-series-forward/

5. "Becoming irresistible," *Deloitte Review*, 2015.

6. Ibid.

7. Ibid.

8. Simon Sinek, "How Great Leaders Inspire Action," TEDx, Puget Sound, September 2009, ted.com/talks/simon_sinek_how_great_leaders_inspire_action

9. Laura Kutsch, "Can We Rely on Our Intuition?" *Scientific American*, August 15, 2019, scientificamerican.com/article/can-we-rely-on-our-intuition/

10. Amanda Rajkumar speaks with Adam Grant on podcast, "Introducing Forward."

11. Based on interviews with DE&I leaders from SAP customer organizations across the globe, conducted by SAP SuccessFactors HR Research Team, 2020–2021.

12. Ibid.

13. Ibid.

14. "Portugal: New Rules Establishing Quotas for Disabled Workers in Portugal," L&E Global, January 29, 2019, knowledge.leglobal. org/portugal-new-rules-establishing-quotas-for-disabled-workers-in-portugal/

15. "Denmark," European Institute for Gender Equality, eige.europa .eu/gender-mainstreaming/countries/denmark

16. hec.europa.eu/commission/presscorner/detail/en/ip_21_881

17. Based on interviews with DE&I leaders.

Chapter 6: I Value You: Belief, Recognition, Appreciation

1. Ian Spelling, "Best Ted Lasso Quotes: 18 Inspiring Pieces of Coaching Wisdom," Fatherly.com, July 16, 2021, fatherly.com/play/best-ted-lasso-quotes/
2. Brené Brown interviews Jason Sudeikis about Ted Lasso, brenebrown.com, October 7, 2020, brenebrown.com/podcast/brene-with-jason-sudeikis-brendan-hunt-on-ted-lasso/
3. John Hagel III, John Seely Brown, and Lang Davison, "Are All Employees Knowledge Workers?" *Harvard Business Review*, April 5, 2010, hbr.org/2010/04/are-all-employees-knowledge-wo.html
4. Ibid.
5. Ibid.
6. Ibid.
7. James M. Citrin and Darleen Derosa, *Leading at a Distance*, Wiley, 2001, pp. 67–68.
8. "Becoming Irresistible: A New Model for Employee Engagement," *Deloitte Review*, Issue 16, January 27, 2015, www2.deloitte.com/us/en/insights/deloitte-review/issue-16/employee-engagement-strategies.html
9. Ibid.
10. Claire Hastwell, "Creating a Culture of Recognition," Great PlaceToWork.com, September 9, 2021, greatplacetowork.com/resources/blog/creating-a-culture-of-recognition

Chapter 7: Authentic Beats Perfect: Leadership Today

1. Brené Brown, "Trust in Emergence: Grounded Theory and My Research Process," brenebrown.com/the-research/
2. Adam Grant, *Original: How Non-Conformists Move the World*, Viking, 2016, p. 82.

3. Janet Britcher, "Replace Micromanaging with Macromanaging for Leadership Success," Forbes.com, February 26, 2018, forbes.com/sites/forbescoachescouncil/2018/02/26/replace-micromanaging-with-macromanaging-for-leadership-success

4. Claire Hastwell, "The 6 Elements of Great Company Culture," Great Place to Work, August 19, 2021, greatplacetowork.com/resources/blog/6-elements-of-great-company-culture

Chapter 8: Collaboration at Work: Humane Technology

1. Evelyn Cheng, "$24 million iced tea company says it's pivoting to the blockchain, and its stock jumps 200%," CNBC.com, December 26, 2017, cnbc.com/2017/12/21/long-island-iced-tea-micro-cap-adds-blockchain-to-name-and-stock-soars.html

2. Thomas Suddendorf, *The Gap: The Science of What Separates Us from Other Animals*, Basic, 2013.

3. Erica Volini, Indranil Roy, Maren Hauptmann, Yves Van Durme, "From Jobs to Superjobs" (term "superjobs" coined by Deloitte), Deloitte Insights, April 11, 2019, www2.deloitte.com/us/en/insights/focus/human-capital-trends/2019/impact-of-ai-turning-jobs-into-superjobs.html

4. Susan Lund, James Manyika, Liz Hilton Segel, André Dua, Bryan Hancock, Scott Rutherford, and Brent Macon, "The Future of Work in America: People and Places, Today and Tomorrow," McKinsey & Company, July 11, 2019, mckinsey.com/featured-insights/future-of-work/the-future-of-work-in-america-people-and-places-today-and-tomorrow

5. Brian A. Primack, Ariel Shensa, Jaime E. Sidani, Erin O. Whaite, Liu Yi Lin, Daniel Rosen, Jason B. Colditz, Ana Radovic, and Elizabeth Miller, "Social Media Use and Perceived Social Isolation Among Young Adults in the U.S.," AJPM, March 6, 2017; "The Social Dilemma: Social Media and Your Mental Health," McLean Hospital, February 9, 2021, mcleanhospital.org/essential/it-or-not-social-medias-affecting-your-mental-health

6. Steve Hunt, "Stupid, Ineffective, and Cruel: The human cost of bad employee self-service technology experiences," LinkedIn, March 20, 2019, linkedin.com/pulse/stupid-ineffective-cruel-human-cost-bad-employee-technology-hunt/

7. Dr. Mary Hayes, Dr. Frances Chumney, and Marcus Buckingham, "The HRXPS: How to measure the performance and impact of HR through the lens of the employee experience," AP Research Institute, 2021, page 27, adpri.org/wp-content/uploads/2021/09/25102402/R0150_0921_v1_HRXPS_ResearchReport.pdf

8. Brian Kropp, "9 Trends That Will Shape Work in 2021 and Beyond," *Harvard Business Review*, January 14, 2021, hbr.org/2021/01/9-trends-that-will-shape-work-in-2021-and-beyond

9. "Becoming Irresistible: A New Model for Employee Engagement," *Deloitte Review*, Issue 16, January 27, 2015, www2.deloitte.com/us/en/insights/deloitte-review/issue-16/employee-engagement-strategies.html

Chapter 9: Thriving at Work: A Focus on Health

1. Jen Fisher speaks with Adam Grant on podcast, "Introducing Forward," news.sap.com/2021/10/introducing-sap-original-series-forward/

2. Seana Smith, "Nearly 80% of US Workers Are Concerned about Their Mental Health as Burnout Skyrockets: Survey," Yahoo! Finance, October 7, 2021, finance.yahoo.com/news/nearly-80-of-us-workers-are-concerned-about-their-mental-health-as-burnout-skyrockets-survey-145759958.html

3. Ibid.

4. Courtney Reum, "Why Arianna Huffington Says Burnout Shouldn't Be the Price of Startup Success," M13.co, m13.co/article/arianna-huffington-why-burnout-shouldnt-be-the-price-of-startup-success

5. Arthur C. Brooks, "'Success Addicts' Choose Being Special Over Being Happy," *The Atlantic*, July 30, 2020, theatlantic.com/family/archive/2020/07/why-success-wont-make-you-happy/614731/

6. "How to Promote Well Being and Tackle the Causes of Work-Related Mental Health Problems," Mind.org.uk, mind.org.uk/media-a/4808/how-to-promote-wellbeing-and-tackle-the-causes-of-work-related-mh-problems_walesv2.pdf

7. Naz Beheshti, "10 Timely Statistics About the Connection Between Employee Connection and Wellness," Forbes.com, January 16, 2019, forbes.com/sites/nazbeheshti/2019/01/16/10-timely-statistics-about-the-connection-between-employee-engagement-and-wellness; apa.org/news/press/releases/2016/06/workplace-well-being

8. Brian Kopp, Alexia Cambon, and Sara Clark, "What Does It Mean to Be a Manager Today?" *Harvard Business Review*, April 15, 2021, hbr.org/2021/04/what-does-it-mean-to-be-a-manager-today

9. The Power of Peloton, Now for Business, onepeloton.com/corporate-wellness

10. "2019 Health and Financial Wellbeing Mindset Study: The state of employee wellbeing," Alight, alight.com/research-insights/state-of-employee-wellbeing-2019

Chapter 10: The Results Are In: Productivity and Efficiency

1. Jill Popelka, "Thrive XM Index 2020 Report: The Case for Employee Experience Driving Business Results," SAP, October 7, 2020, news.sap.com/2020/10/thrive-xm-study-2020-employee-experience-business-results/

2. Brian Kopp, "9 Trends That Will Shape Work in 2021 and Beyond," *Harvard Business Review*, January 14, 2021, hbr.org/2021/01/9-trends-that-will-shape-work-in-2021-and-beyond

3. Jason Wingard, "Remote Working: How to Succeed Over the Long Term," Forbes.com, May 22, 2020, forbes.com/sites/jasonwingard/2020/05/22/remote-working-how-to-succeed-over-the-long-term

4. "Gartner HR Survey Reveals 41% of Employees Likely to Work Remotely at Least Some of the Time Post Coronavirus

Pandemic," Gartner, April 14, 2020, gartner.com/en/newsroom/press-releases/2020-04-14-gartner-hr-survey-reveals-41--of-employees-likely-to-

5. "Becoming Irresistible: A New Model for Employee Engagement," *Deloitte Review*, Issue 16, January 27, 2015, www2.deloitte.com/us/en/insights/deloitte-review/issue-16/employee-engagement-strategies.html

6. "The Power of Story," interview with Jim Loehr, IdeaConnection, ideaconnection.com/interviews/00009-The-Power-of-Story.html

7. "How Adidas Promotes Diversity, Equity, and Inclusion in the Workplace," Forbes.com, November 10, 2021, forbes.com/sites/sap/2021/11/10/how-adidas-promotes-diversity-equity-and-inclusion-in-the-workplace

8. Lisa Christensen, Jake Gittleson, Matt Smith, and Heather Stefanski, "Reviving the Art of Apprenticeship to Unlock Continuous Skill Development," McKinsey & Company, October 21, 2021, mckinsey.com/business-functions/people-and-organizational-performance/our-insights/reviving-the-art-of-apprenticeship-to-unlock-continuous-skill-development

9. Kevin Roose, "Sorry, but Working from Home Is Overrated," *The New York Times*, March 10, 2020, nytimes.com/2020/03/10/technology/working-from-home.html

10. Ibid.

11. Ibid.

Chapter 11: Keep the Pace: Agility and Resilience

1. "Becoming Irresistible: A New Model for Employee Engagement," *Deloitte Review*, Issue 16, January 27, 2015, www2.deloitte.com/us/en/insights/deloitte-review/issue-16/employee-engagement-strategies.html

2. "Changes in the American workplace," Pew Research Center, October 6, 2016, pewresearch.org/social-trends/2016/10/06/1-changes-in-the-american-workplace/

3. "Becoming Irresistible," 2015.

4. Adam Grant, *Think Again*, Viking, 2021, p. 209.

5. Ibid.

6. Adam Grant Twitter, January 29, 2021, twitter.com/adammgrant/status/1355144932659523593

7. David Johnson, "Why High Performance People Need High Performance Technology," Forrester, April 2, 2016, forrester.com/blogs/16-04-02-why_high_performance_people_need_high_performance_technology/

8. Stephanie Kasriel, "Skill, Re-skill and Re-skill Again: How to keep up with the future of work," World Economic Forum, July 31, 2017, weforum.org/agenda/2017/07/skill-reskill-prepare-for-future-of-work/

9. "Becoming Irresistible," 2015.

10. "Why It's Important to Upskill and Reskill Your Workforce," SAP Insights, insights.sap.com/importance-upskilling/

Chapter 12: Sustainable Growth for People *and* Business

1. Tsedal Neeley, *Remote Work Revolution: Succeeding from Anywhere*, Harper Business, 2021, p. 156.

2. Ibid., p. 118.

3. Ibid., p. 37.

4. Deirdre Lockwood, "Most People Can't Work from Home," DEOHS School of Public Health, University of Washington, April 8, 2020, deohs.washington.edu/hsm-blog/most-people-cant-work-home

5. Mary Ellen Slayter, "Q&A: How the Work of Tomorrow Compares to the Work of Today: Interview with Thomas Kochan," Monster.com, monster.com/career-advice/article/future-work-thomas-kochan-interview

6. "Measuring Stakeholder Capitalism: Toward Common Metrics and Consistent Reporting of Sustainable Value Creation,"

World Economic Forum, September 2020, www3.weforum
.org/docs/WEF_IBC_Measuring_Stakeholder_Capitalism_
Report_2020.pdf

7. Joe Tenebruso, "5 Great Quotes from Starbucks CEO Howard
Schultz," The Motley Fool, June 26, 2015, fool.com/investing/
general/2015/06/26/5-great-quotes-from-starbucks-ceo-howard-
schultz.aspx

Storm Home

1. archive.attn.com/stories/12673/difference-between-working-
now-and-thirty-years-ago

2. Jen Fisher speaks with Adam Grant on podcast, Introducing
Forward, https://news.sap.com/2021/10/introducing-sap-original-
series-forward/

Acknowledgments

Today I am grateful to be surrounded by true geniuses at work, and we all know that people are the most essential part of any experience. In writing this book I am so grateful to have had these people beside me: Sam Yerks, Rory Pumilia, Melanie Stevens, Meg Bear, Amy Wilson, Scott Lietzke, Maryann Abbajay, Autumn Krauss, Lauren Bidwell, Toshiaki Inagaki, Sushant Jain, Jay Choi, Frances Botha, David Boyle, and Michael Ciocia. Without their contributions, you would not be reading this right now.

Steve Hunt, thank you: Several sections of this book directly or indirectly reflect your insights, stories, and observations.

Courtney Kimbrough, you kept the whole ship sailing. You kept us calm in times of stress, you challenged us when it was needed, and your deep knowledge of HR and international cultures helped bring the ideas and thoughts to life in a very real way.

Andy Postman, you have taught me so much in this process, you made us laugh, and you are truly a master of your trade. Evan Leatherwood, thank you for your encouragement and guidance.

Zach Schisgal and the team at Wiley: You have been invaluable in the journey to bring *Experience, Inc.* to the world. I am so grateful for your partnership.

I cannot leave without thanking the people who have been cheering me along from the start of this project: Raedean

Popelka, Mindy Popelka, Lana Wood, Carol Pimpler, Franklin Kohutek, Bill Lawson, Giora Barker, Daniella Bowling, and Ayo Adedipe. There are many people who have impacted my beliefs and understanding of experience. These people challenge me and provide a storm home when I need it.

Kalie, Cole, and Jimmy, thank you for giving me purpose and joy, for challenging me, and for believing in me. YOU are the greatest part of this life experience.

About the Author

Jill Popelka is a senior executive leader for global software company SAP. A believer that purpose drives people and people drive business performance, Jill studies the impact of employee experience on organizations and how to maximize potential for employees and employers. In her debut book, *Experience, Inc.*, she brings to life the stories of workers from across regions, industries, and roles.

Jill lives in Texas with her husband, Jimmy, their children, Kalie and Cole, and the family's spirited Boston Terrier, Beckett.

Index

For more resources
on employee experience
and the future of business,
visit **insights.sap.com**.

To learn more about
SAP SuccessFactors Human
Experience Management
Suite, visit **SAP.com/HR**.

Engage with the author at jillpopelka.com   in @jillpopelka